To Alice Hohenberg Federico

Salvatore Federico

Paintings

Edward Lucie Smith

Walter Wickiser Gallery, Inc., Publisher

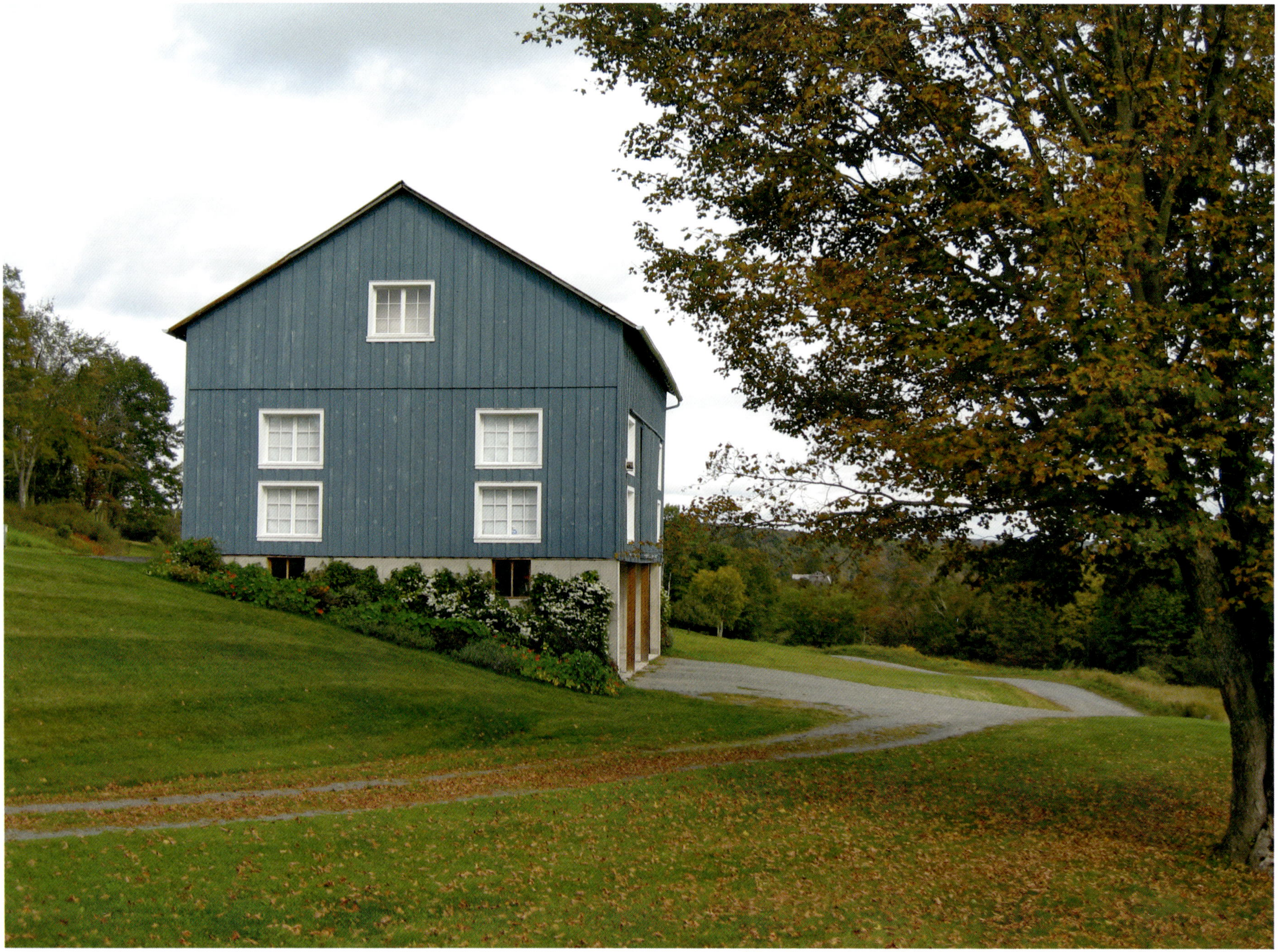

Barn studio near Jeffersonville New York, 2017

SALVATORE FEDERICO

PAINTINGS

EDWARD LUCIE SMITH

WALTER WICKISER GALLERY, INC., PUBLISHER

Editor: Walter Wickiser

Designer: Ji Min Hwang

Color Editor: Yolanda Feng

Library of Congress Control Number: 2019903467

ISBN: 978-0-578-48306-1

Published in 2019 by Walter Wickiser Gallery, Incorporated, New York

WALTER WICKISER GALLERY INC.
210 Eleventh Avenue Suite 303
New York, NY 10001
www.walterwickisergallery.com
wwickiserg@aol.com

COVER:

OLAF, 2007, 73" x 65", ACRYLIC ON CANVAS

Contents

Salvatore Federico Paintings

By Edward Lucie-Smith

Salvatore Federico has had a long and distinguished artistic career, and the paintings he is now making are instantly recognisable as his. He creates boldly energetic abstract compositions, but somewhere within these designs there are what one might describe as gestures towards the idea of figuration. He was indeed at one time a figurative painter. Towards the end of the 1980s he was still making some figurative works.

Where his work differs most markedly from that of the abstracts being produced by other American masters, of the same, or a somewhat earlier generation, is in its expression of energy. All vestiges of figuration have fallen away. His current paintings are best described as boldly energetic symbols, or signs. Symbols of what?

If one looks at the abstractions made by some of the great names of the past, one notes that they tend to fall into two groups. In one group, the forms are essentially stable. Rothko's colour blocks float serenely, one above the other. Mondrian's grids do not suggest the possibility of movement. Where movement is suggested, as it is in Pollock's so-called 'drip paintings', the whole painted surface seems to move. Federico's recent work does neither of these things.

Each work presents the viewer with a sign, crisply rendered on a ground of contrasting colour, or else on black. In paintings made a little earlier than those presented here, there are sometimes groups of signs, not just a single one. And where a sign appears singly, there is often, still, a hint of figurative reference. You can, if you insist, see the form as a bird, or else. In two cases at least, you perceive a highly simplified version of the famous Ancient Egyptian bust of Nefertiti, now in a museum in Berlin.

Salvatore Federico, Barn Studio, 2017

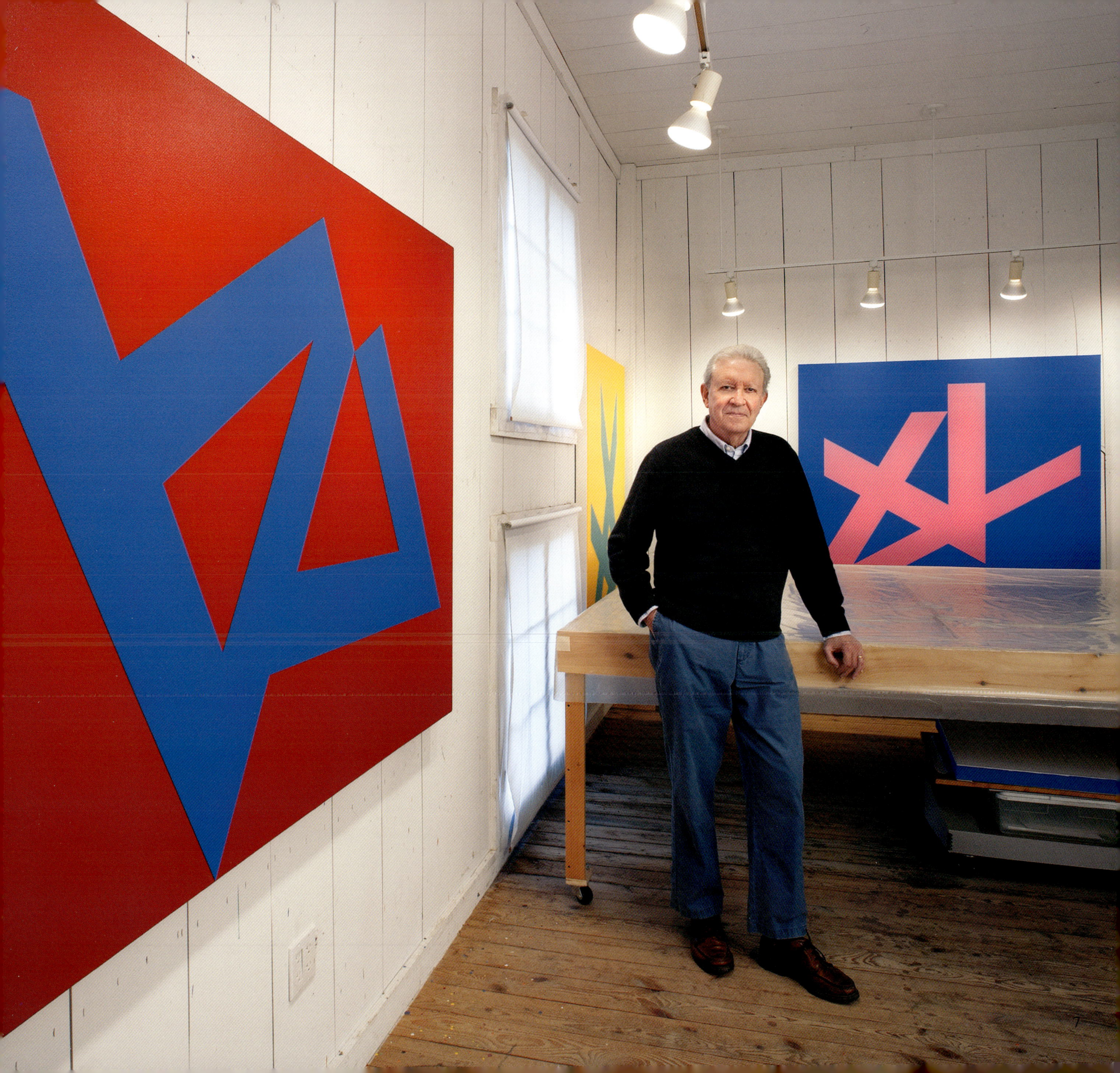

None of these subdued hints of figuration survive in Federico's most recent work. Each painting now presents a single authoritative image, though often one with complex boundaries. This image is rendered using a single hue, without interior modelling, against a ground of contrasting hue which, in turn, is equally flat.

These big signs have something in common with contemporary commercial art–which is to say, with the commercial culture of billboards and large-scale advertisements that produced the Pop Art of the 1960s. They also have elements in common with things that are much more remote: with, for example, the hermetic symbols on encounters in ancient alchemical texts, or–still further–back, with some of the graffiti that speleologists encounter in long-ago inhabited caves. We know these signs have meaning, but they challenge us to interpret them.

The wider relevance here is the role and significance of a purely abstract art in relationship to contemporary society. If one looks at the history of art–art seen through western eyes in the context of western society–during the course of the 20th century, what one seems to see at first is a struggle to separate art from the need to convey any kind of social or political message. Art was to be a thing in itself, operating entirely within its own realm of reference. These attitudes reached a kind of climax in the Minimal Art of the 1970s. It is of course self-evident, if one looks at Federico's work, that he was never part of this.

Looking more closely, one discovers that supposedly non political abstract art did very often carry a freight of social and political meanings. This was especially the case with Abstract Expressionism, the art movement that made American art triumphant throughout the western world. Abstract Expressionism came to be seen as the expression of American individualism, as opposed to the constraints imposed on artists by the rulers of the Soviet Union. The American artist could speak out, expose his or her inner consciousness, without constraint. This message was propagated in touring exhibitions sent to Europe with the backing of the Museum of Modern Art in New York and also, hovering in the shadows, that of the CIA.

If one looks at the parallel history of visual art in the Soviet Union, one sees a very different pattern.

In the years just before and immediately after the Russian Revolution of 1917, which brought the Communist Party to power, one does indeed see the apparent triumph of abstract art, as personified by Malevich, but one also notes how quickly this impulse was suppressed. The suppression succeeded, in part at least, because of the existence of a strong tradition of socially engaged art in Russia, dating from the later decades of the 19th century embodied by the group of Pre-Revolutionary artists called the Peredvizhniki or Wanderers. The fact was that Russian art of the early revolutionary years already had an experimental tradition quite different from that which was proposed by Futurist abstraction, and this accommodated itself more easily to the wishes of the new regime without necessarily being always conformist.

Recent exhibitions commemorating the Russian Revolution, for example the one held in 2017 by the Royal Academy in London, tended to show, perhaps without really meaning to do so, how quickly Futurism in Russia came to a full stop, especially in its most abstract guise. That tradition has never been fully revived in contemporary Russian art, even after the fall, some two decades ago, of Soviet rule in Russia.

Federico's current work must, therefore, be thought of as being isolated from either of these two established traditions–one derived essentially from Abstract Expressionism in America, and the other, more remotely, from Futurist abstract art in Russia. It does not make statements that are directly relevant to either, and this, paradoxically, is part of its strength.

What it does is to propose a new kind of relationship between contemporary abstract art and the society around it. Something that is almost never noted, in discussions about 20th century abstraction is the effect it has had on other kinds of visual communication. In particular, on the way these are read by their audience. If one looks at photography in particular, what one sees is a kind of visual communication that is sometimes classified, or classifies itself, as a form of what we call "art." And which sometimes rejects that description.

When it is 'art'–a means of creating images for their own sake–it sometimes attempts to escape from making anything that offers parallels to anything that can be observed in the external, visible world. Quite often, this means abandoning any use of a lens and choosing to experiment instead simply with materials and processes that are associated with the making of photographic prints.

Commercial photography–photographic images used as a powerful means of selling things, which is to say images used as tools, not for their own sake-has pursued a course of its own. The invention of abstract art, as a Western genre, affected both art itself, and the way in which the audience for art, the recipients of these new, would-be independent images, looked at the world surrounding them. This is to say that the audience, the people who looked, became more and more aware, though often perhaps not wholly consciously, of the abstract shapes underlying familiar scenes and objects. Abstract art became a tutor, which taught them to look at the world in a new way.

Anyone who looks at modern advertising now is, whether they choose to acknowledge it or not, a beneficiary of this process. If one looks at the advertising imagery produced in the past and then at what confronts one now, one surely becomes aware of how much this act of looking has changed. Also, very often, especially for urban populations, of how much the process has speeded up.

I think it is this situation that Federico both recognises and challenges in this most recent series of paintings.

The images they present are certainly not what aficionados of contemporary art will immediately recognise as Pop Art, a movement that arose to challenge the values espoused by the Abstract Expressionism that immediately preceded it in the art of the United States. Yet the paintings do undoubtedly have certain underlying characteristics in common with things familiar from typical Pop paintings–notably the use of clear-cut images against plain, uninflected fields of colour. Instead of offering a portrait of a film star, or one of a can of Campbell's soup, they offer mysterious signs.

Sometimes these can seem like large glyphs from an unknown language, simultaneously offering meaning and yet at the same time defiantly withholding it. This combination of opposing characteristics, being at the same time open and mysterious, makes them seem both familiar and yet, at the same time, stubbornly withdrawn.

As the Minimal Art movement, which succeeded Pop in the 1970s and early 1980s, has now rather comprehensively demonstrated, art that insists on being art alone, art strictly on its own terms, rapidly runs into limits, once its puritan radicalism becomes simply an inert part of the landscape of contemporary visual art in all its manifestations.

The challenge for purely abstract art now is both to make itself relevant to the spectator and, at the same time, to maintain an element of mystery–to occupy some corner of the mind in the individual who contemplates it and to bring that spectator back to look again.

This is what Federico's recent paintings do, using a deliberately restricted, but still very sophisticated range of technical means. The designs mysteriously change, resonate in a different way, each time you look at them. Looking is what they are about.

– Edward Lucie-Smith 2019

Edward Lucie-Smith is regarded as the most prolific and the most widely published writer on art with more than a hundred books in all and sales for some titles totaling over 250,000 copies. More than sixty of his books are chiefly but not exclusively about contemporary art. Among them "Movements in Art since 1945", "Visual Arts of the 20th Century", "A Dictionary of Art Terms", *and* "Art Today" *are used as standard texts throughout the world. He is internationally acclaimed as an art critic, historian, curator, author, lecturer, poet and photographer. Mr. Lucie-Smith was born in 1933 in Kingston, Jamaica and moved to Britain in 1946. He was educated at King's School, Canterbury and Merton College, Oxford.*

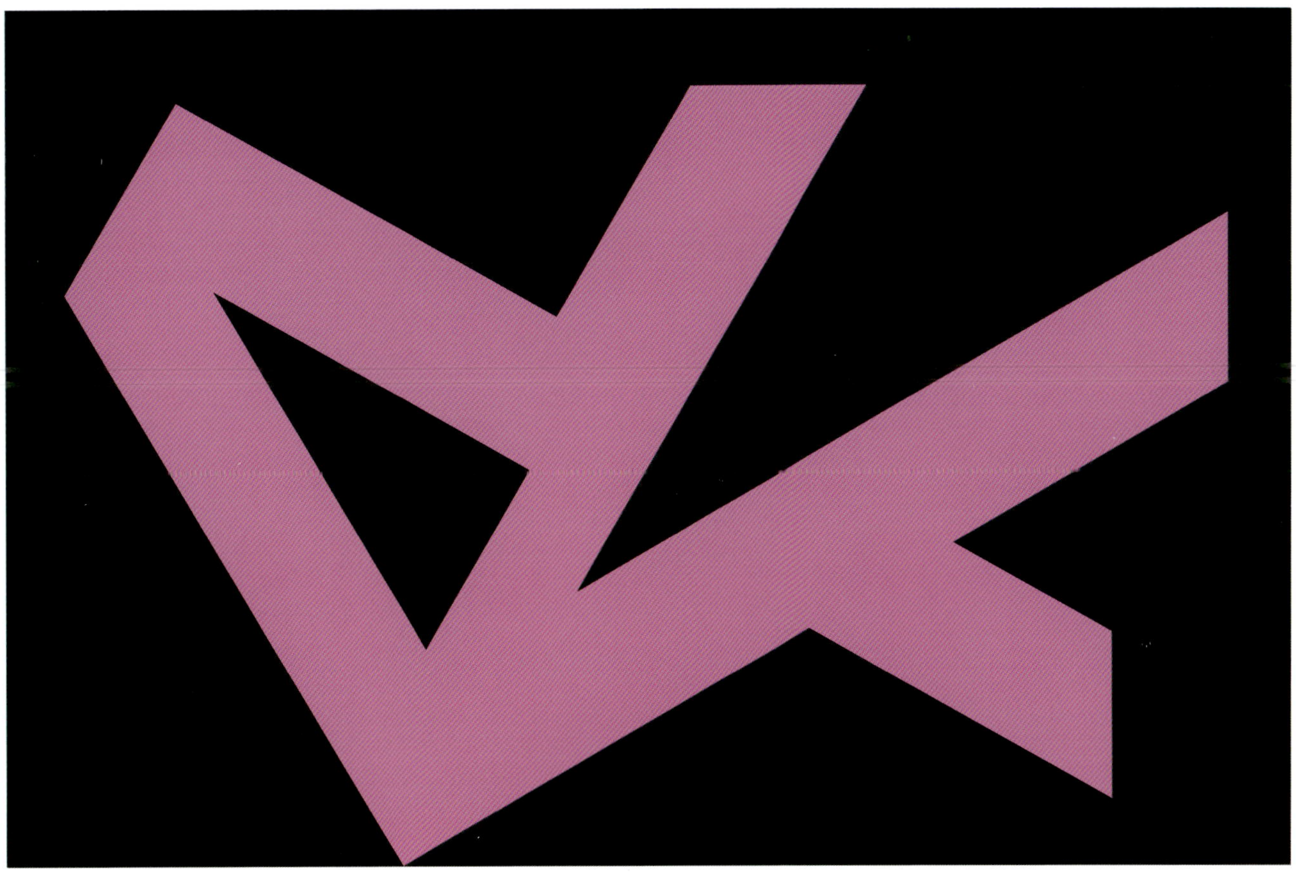

CHIARA, 2018, 37 1/4" x 55 5/8", ACRYLIC ON CANVAS

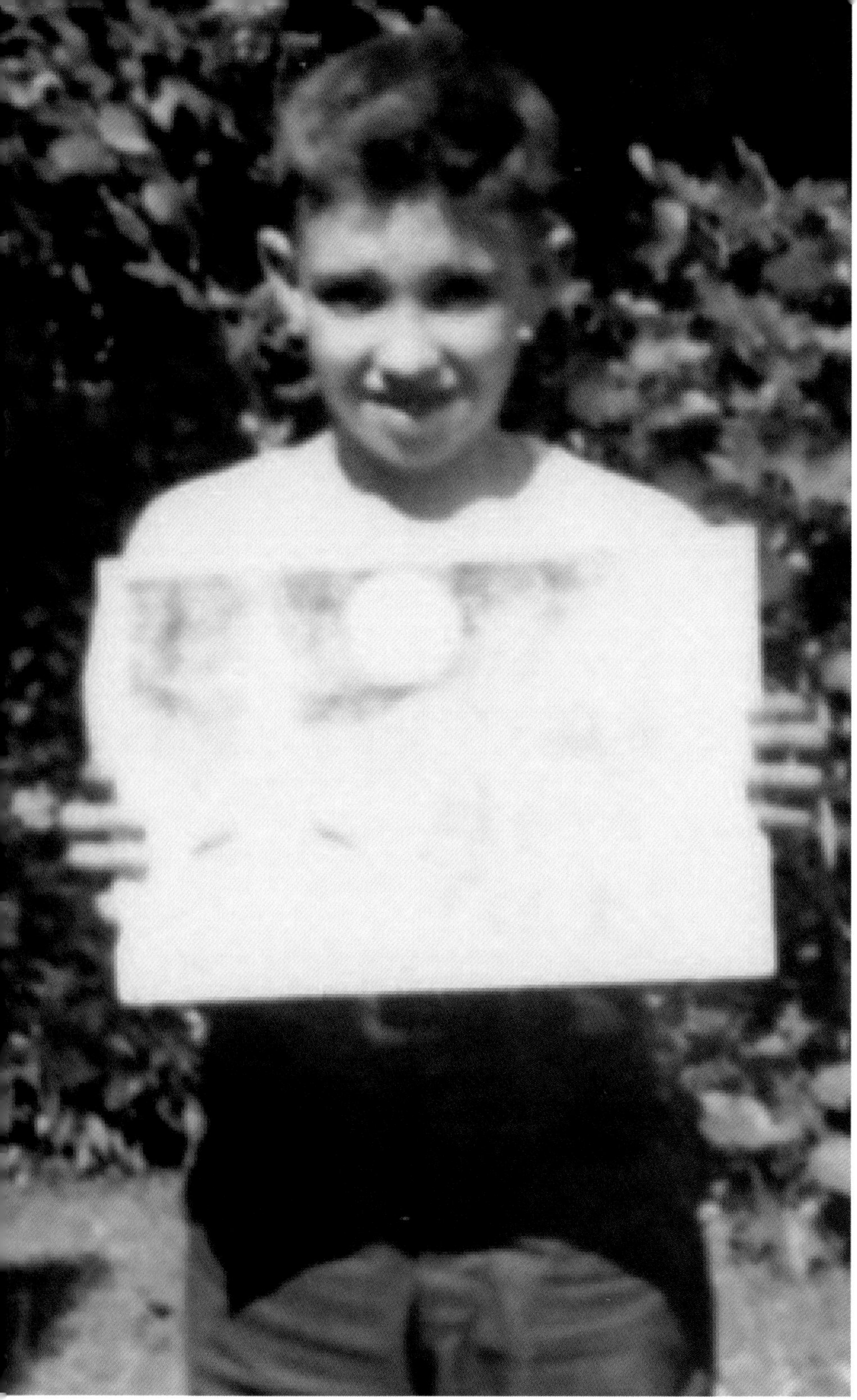

Blue Ribbon Drawing, 1953

SALVATORE FEDERICO (b.1944)

ILLUSTRATIVE HISTORY
BY WALTER WICKISER

Salvatore Federico was born on July 14, 1944 in Washington, D.C., where he lived until age six. His interest in the arts was encouraged from an early age.

When he was four years old, his cousin Anna Colella frequently practiced *"Danza Ritual del Fuego"* by Manuel de Falla on the piano. Federico, sitting beneath the piano, was impressed by the fierce rhythm. Thirty years later, in regular attendance at performances of the New York City Ballet, his vision of the figure in motion was enlarged. Here the music was made visual by the clarity, tension and gesture of the classical dancers. The rhythm, tension, and gestures would make a lasting impact on the direction that Federico's life's work in painting would take.

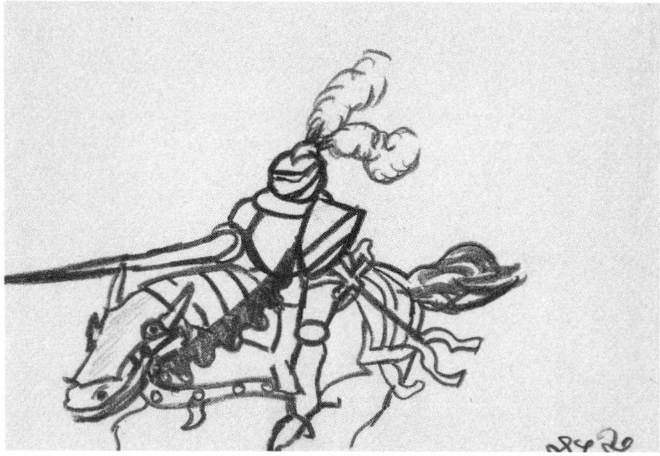

Charging Knight in Armor, 1953

At age five, Federico, accompanied by his Sicilian godmother, visited the National Gallery of Art in Washington for the first time. He long recalled the architecture of the museum and paintings by the old masters. He observed a young woman making a study from one of these paintings. Atop her high stool she looked down at the child and asked, "What would you like to be when you grow up?" Of course, he enthusiastically replied, "I want to be an artist!" She graciously made a gift to him of three of her paintbrushes, which he kept and used throughout art school, years later.

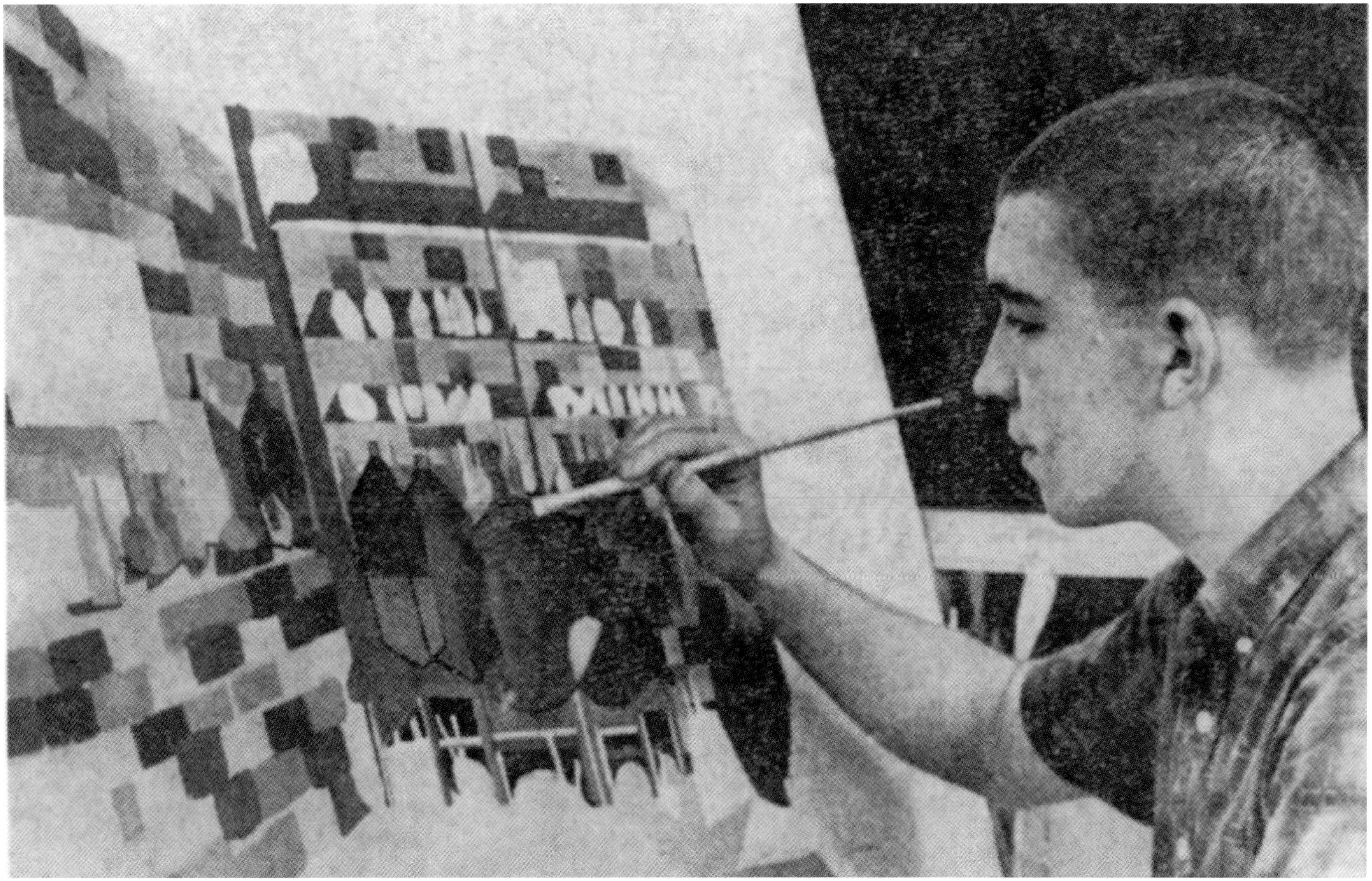

Washington-Lee High School, Arlington, Virginia 1962

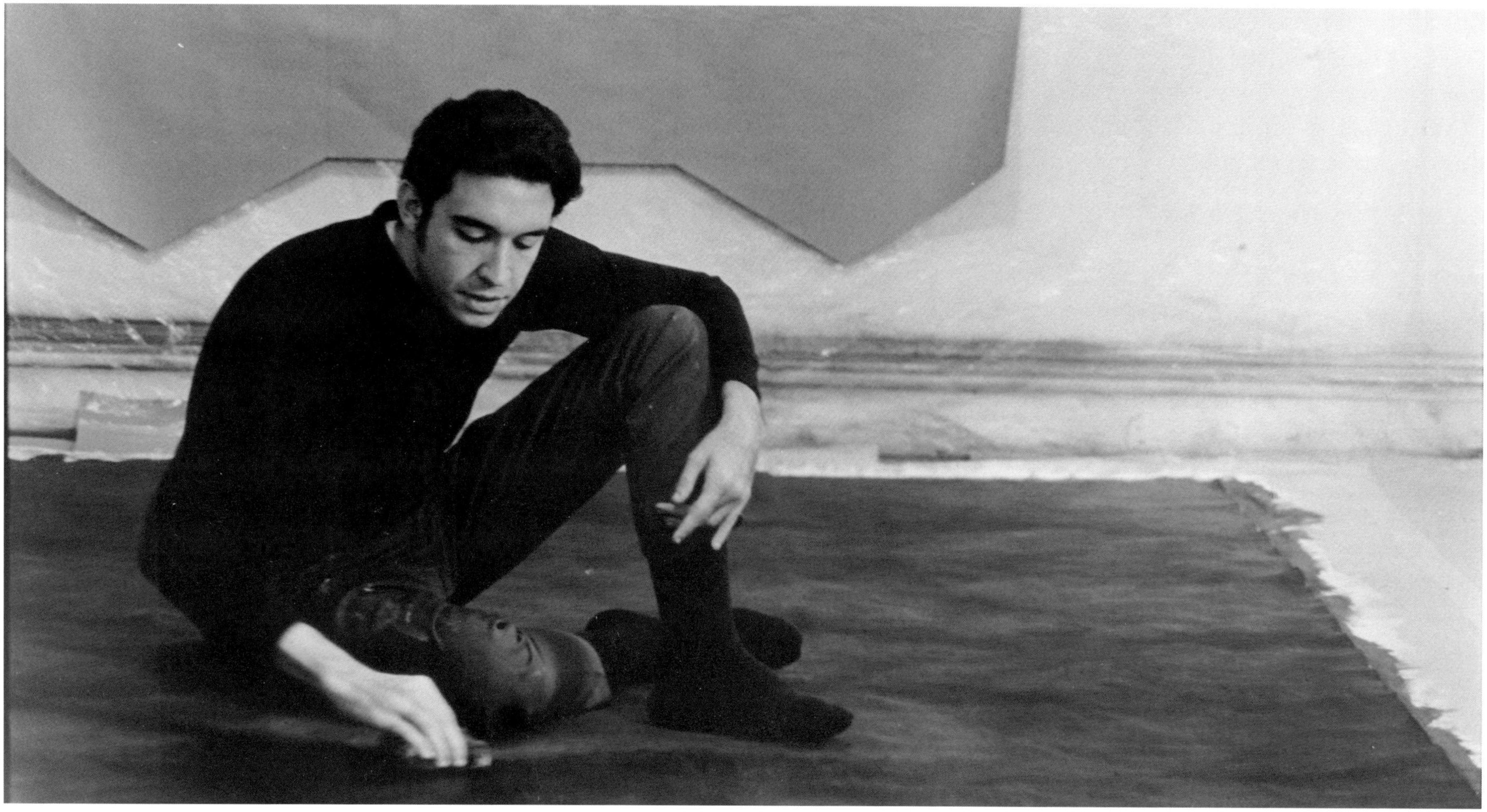

Making Wall-Sized Paintings, 1969

During second grade in elementary school, he made a drawing of a bright, red fire engine in crayon. His teacher proudly put it on display for the next meeting of the Parent-Teacher Association at the school. The next year he won a blue ribbon for one of his landscape drawings. Images of knights in armor, locomotives, and rocket ships followed. His identity as an artist remained as he made his way through the public schools in Arlington, Virginia. He was awarded the gold medal for achievement in the arts during his graduation ceremony at Washington-Lee High School.

Federico received a scholarship to attend the Richmond Professional Institute in Virginia (RPI), where he studied from 1962-1966. Several of his teachers had worked with Hans Hofmann. In his Fundamentals of Drawing class under Jewett Campbell, he created life-size drawings of the human figure in dynamic poses inspired by Michelangelo. Campbell suggested that he might consider more modern artists, such as Picasso or Matisse, to better understand how they viewed figuration among the Renaissance painters. After a symposium at RPI. with artists and writers from New York, Federico first encountered Barnett Newman, in Campbell's studio. Later, certain geometric elements began to appear in his figurative paintings. When his undergraduate work was completed, which included a solo show at the school, he received the BFA degree. He was awarded a Fellowship from the Virginia Museum of Fine Arts to attend Hunter College in NYC.

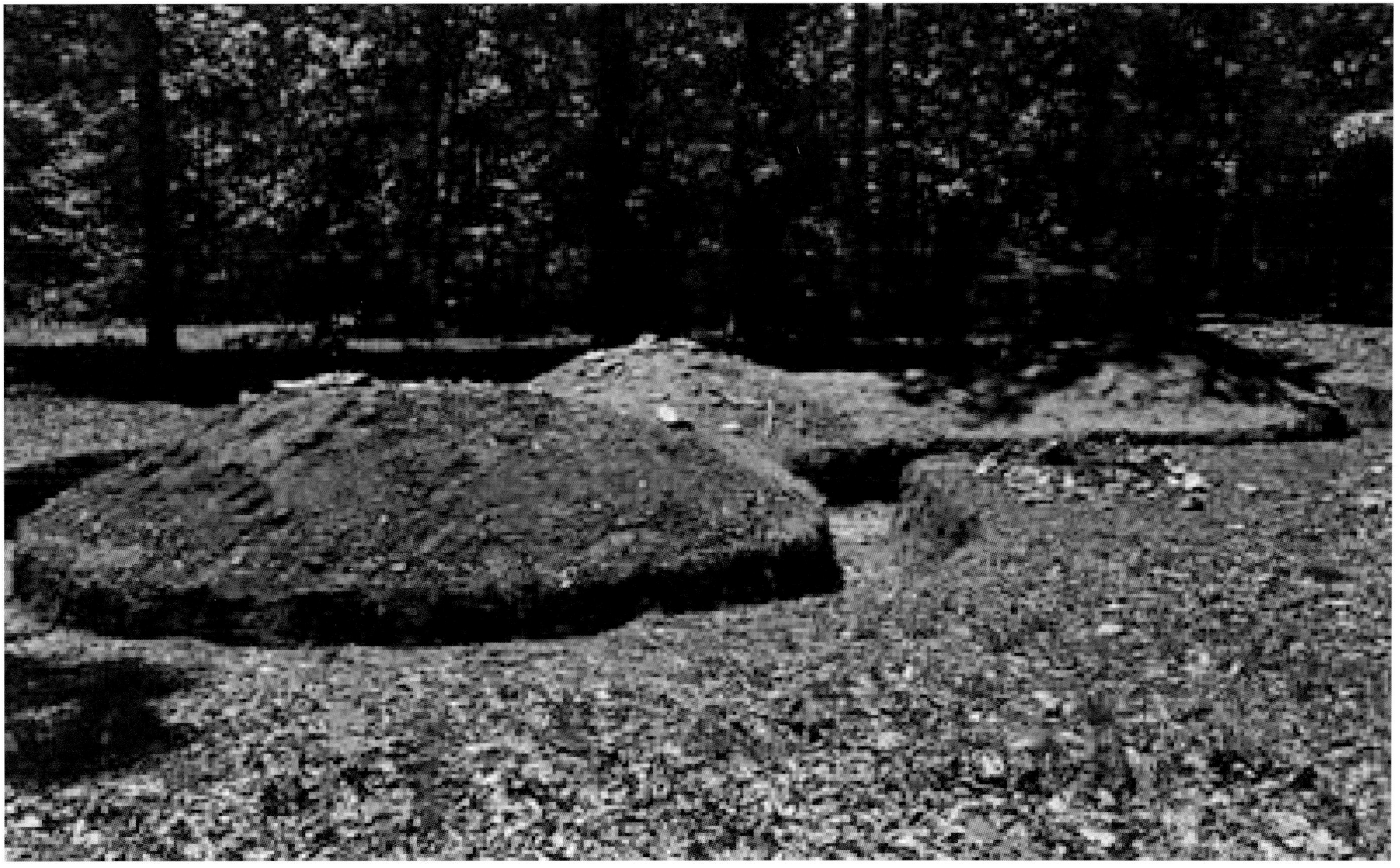

Earthworks, 1967-1968

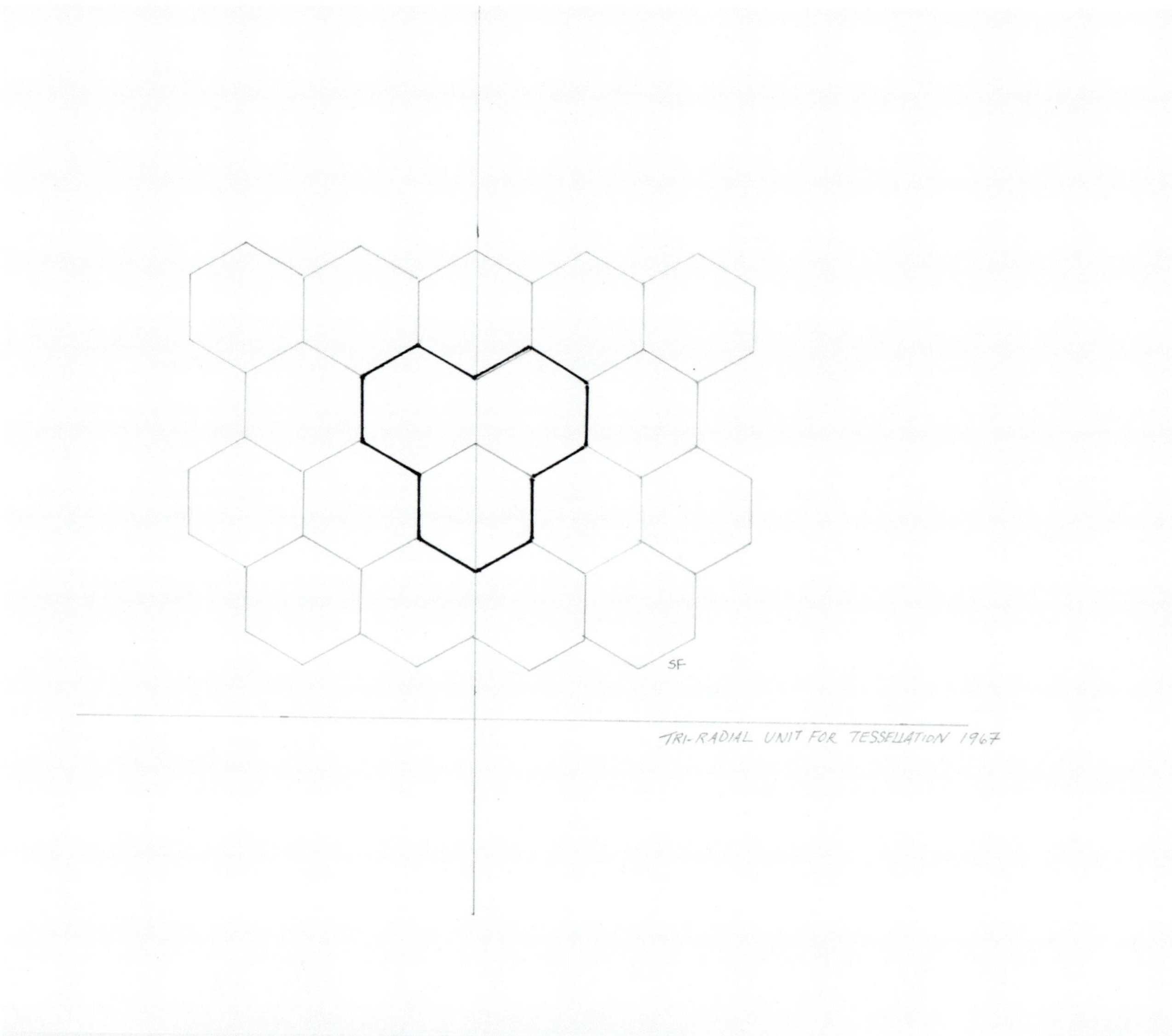

TRI-RADIAL UNIT FOR TESSELLATION, 1967

His coursework at Hunter lasted through the winter of 1966 and the spring of 1967. His thesis advisor was Howard Davis, Art History Chairman at Columbia, who taught a graduate seminar on early Renaissance painting at Hunter. Federico made a presentation to the seminar about the frescoes of Piero della Francesca, with a focus on the stately repetition of visual elements and the graphic impact of heraldry. A dialogue began with Davis, which included the work of contemporary abstract artists. The result was Federico's research paper entitled "Monumentality in Recent American Painting." He received an MA degree in 1971.

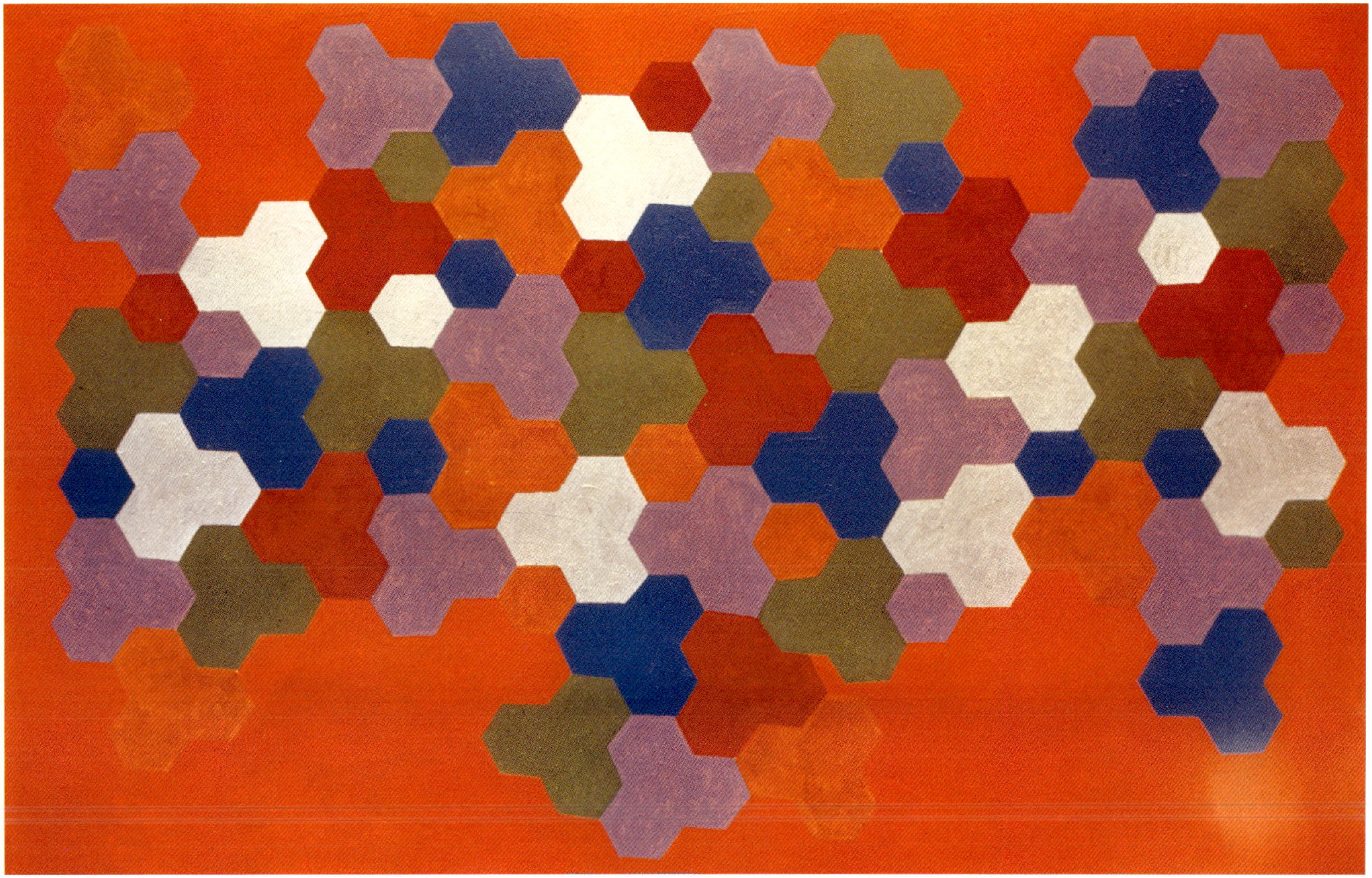

TESSELLATION, 1967, 16" X 24", OIL ON PAPER

At the same time, working with Tony Smith, he discovered a way to make non-figurative forms that embodied gesture and tension through geometry. These early studies anticipated the direction that his work would take in the future. In January 1967, Federico borrowed a book from Smith on the 13 Archimedean Solids-his first encounter with polyhedra. Wanting to understand more throughly these forms, he made templates for tetrahedrons and octahedrons that could be cut out and folded to form solids. He became interested in the configurations of the templates as an end in themselves to form two dimensional shapes for paintings. The use of hexagons, in contrast to equilateral triangles , seemed to promise more possibilities. He made tri-radial shapes from the hexagons and assembled them in an allover configuration within a rectangle (with Pollock in mind). This is how the direction of his life's work began.

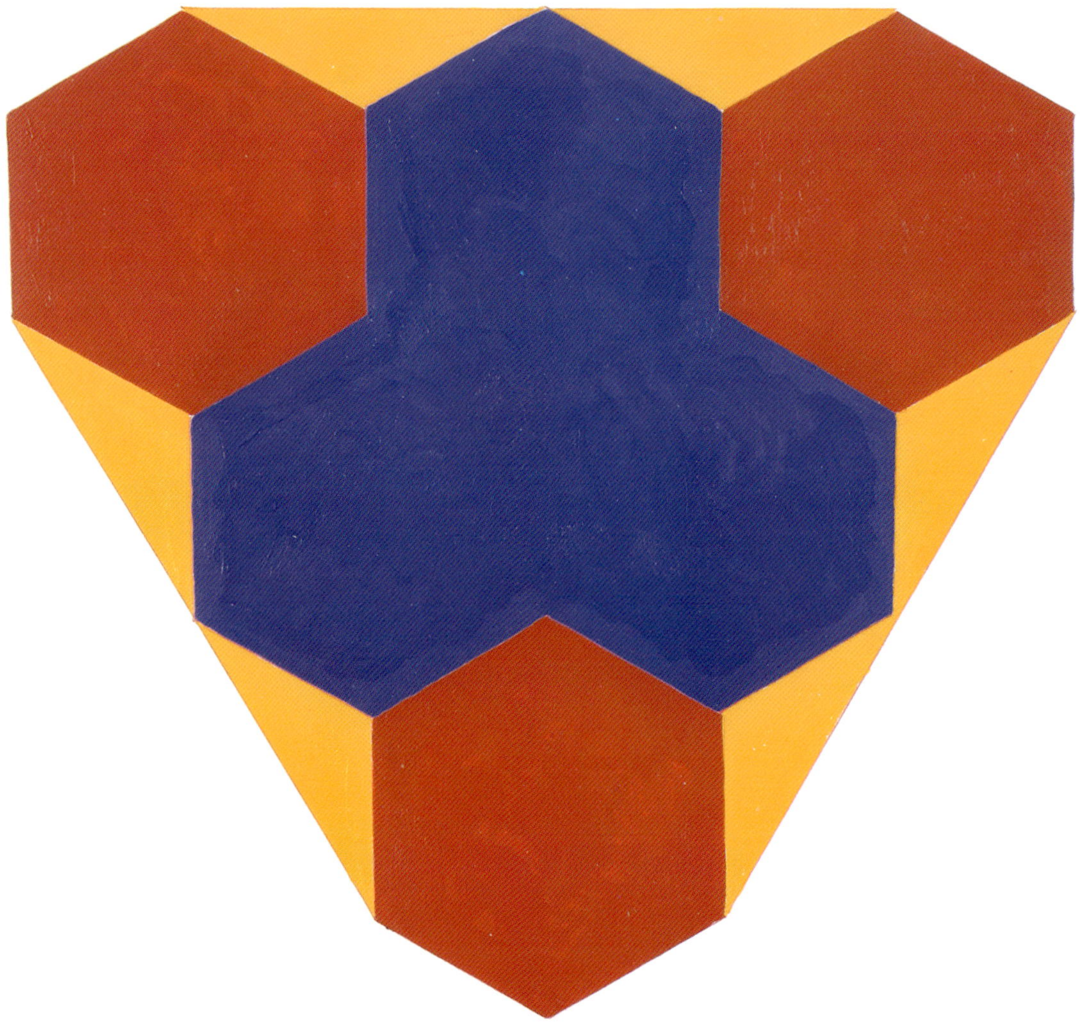

Study for Shaped Canvas, 1967, 10 3/4" x 11 1/2", Acrylic on Paper

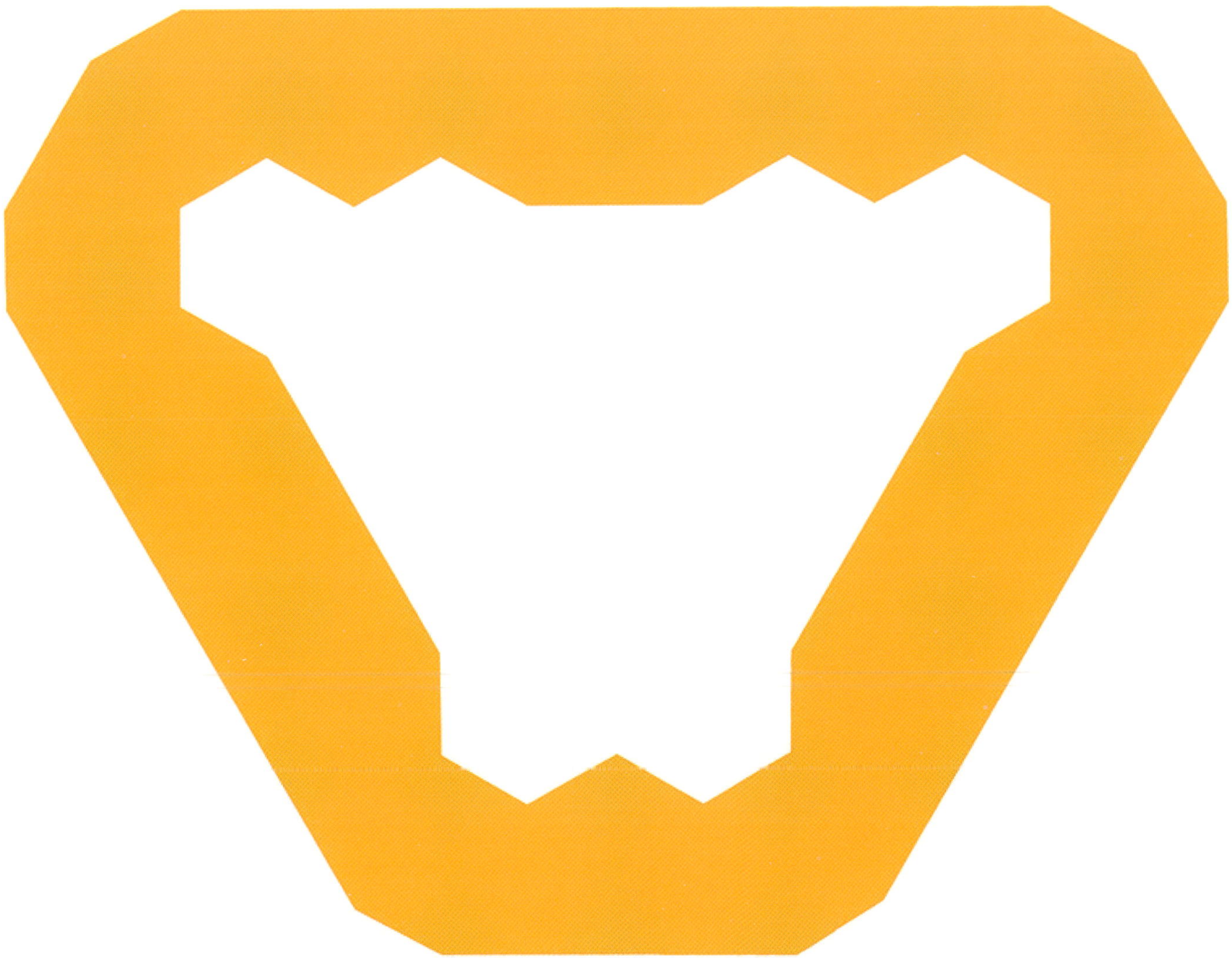

Five O'Clock Shadow, 1970, 84" x 85", Acrylic on Shaped Canvas

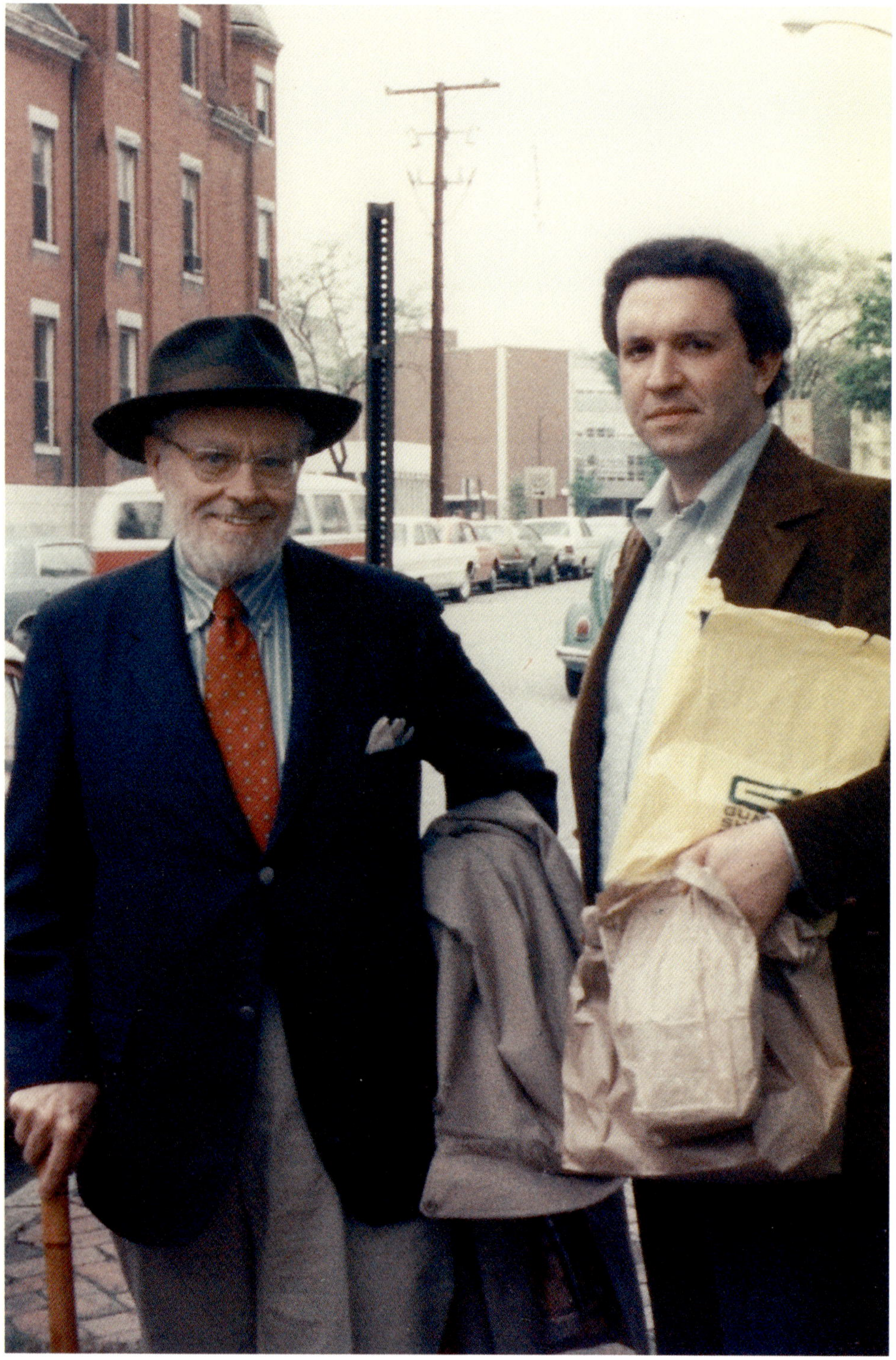

TONY SMITH, SALVATORE FEDERICO 1975

Among the many artists he met during this time was Mark Rothko. After a summer of work in Smith's studio in Orange, New Jersey, Federico began teaching in the autumn of 1967 at Virginia Commonwealth University (VCU).

Joining with several of his colleagues, Painters' Independent Enterprise (P.I.E.) was formed the next year. Underwritten by the well-known arts patrons, Sydney and Frances Lewis, P.I.E. held regular exhibitions at the Carillon Museum, in Richmond, as well as in other venues around the state of Virginia, in Washington, D.C., and at Chapman College in California. Their work attracted the attention of Tom Armstrong, who was serving as director of the Abby Aldrich Rockefeller Folk Art Collection and the Twentieth Century Gallery in Williamsburg. (Armstrong later became the Director of the Whitney Museum). An exhibition of Federico's large geometric paintings was held at the Gallery in 1969.

On her way to the Southeastern Center for Contemporary Art (SECCA) in Winston-Salem, North Carolina, in 1970, the painter Grace Hartigan, an acquaintance among friends in Baltimore, visited Federico's studio in Richmond. Viewing his black & white works on paper, they talked about the graphic power of paintings by her friend, Franz Kline, an artist who had long interested Federico. In 1971, he exhibited one of his recent shaped canvases at SECCA, which received a special notice from the juror and art critic for the New York Times, Hilton Kramer.

Federico remained at VCU, on tenure, until 1975,

when he resigned his teaching position and returned to New York City to pursue his work as a painter. With the exception of a brief period working with graduate students at Ohio State University in 1981, Federico's interest in teaching ended. He found work with Overseas Investors in New York City, and later started a contracting business with a partner, David Feeney, also a painter. After marriage to Alice Hohenberg, a ceramicist, in 1989 he concentrated on his painting.

Consistent with his belief in creative freedom, for a number of years during the 1970s, Federico investigated the possibilities of a more painterly abstraction. Working in his loft on Essex Street in Manhattan (coincidentally Grace Hartigan's old studio), he stretched canvas on the floor and made fields of transparent color that accentuated textural qualities. Applying the paint in parallel rows across the surface resulted in another kind of geometry. His work was encouraged by his friends, Stanley Boxer and Joyce Weinstein, both well-known painters, who introduced him to Jules Olitski and Clement Greenberg. Eventually, Federico added geometric elements of pure color, and he began to make a new series of shaped canvases after he moved his studio to Red Hook in Brooklyn. His large black-and-white works on paper were shown at the Drawing Center in New York City.

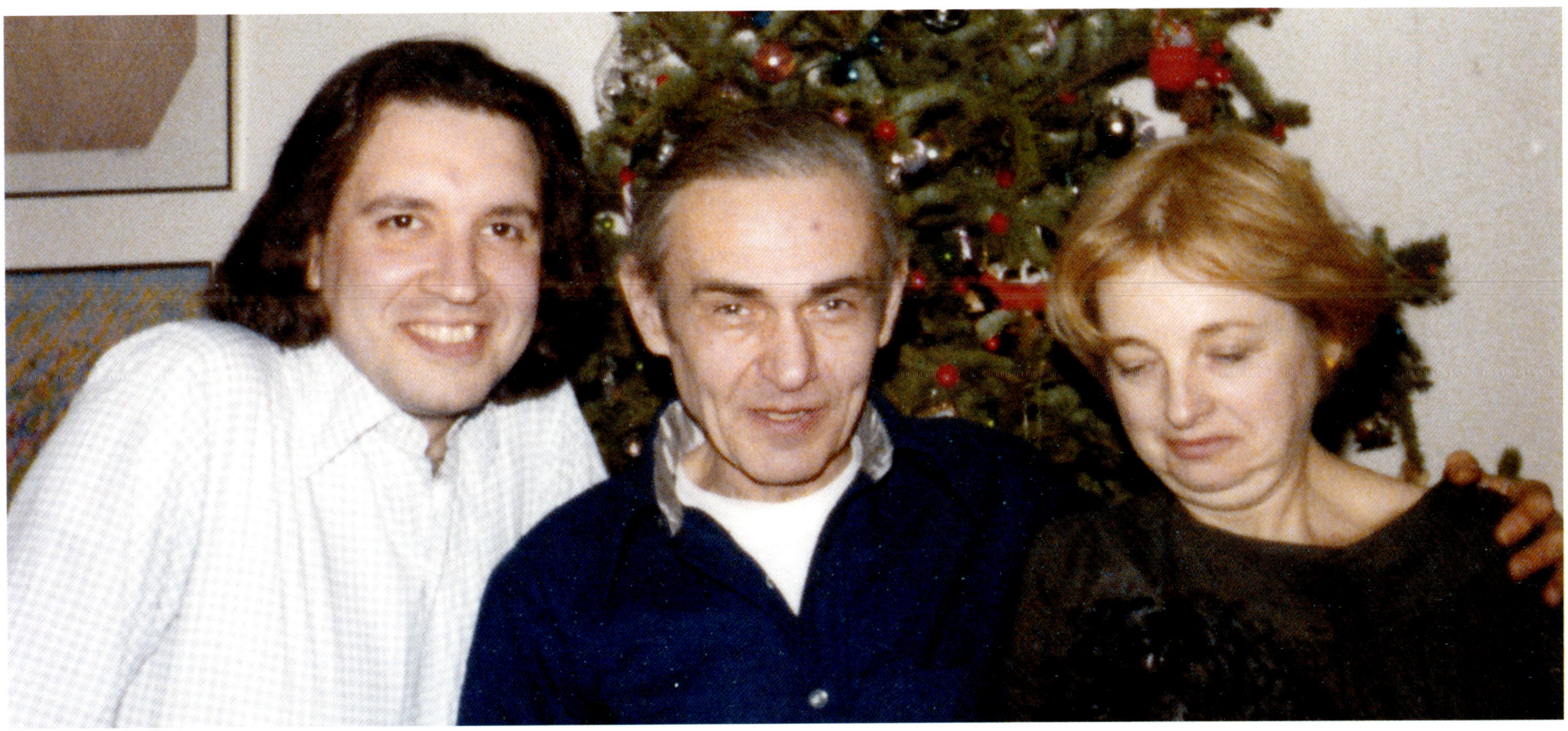

SALVATORE FEDERICO, STANLEY BOXER, JOYCE WEINSTEIN 1977 NYC

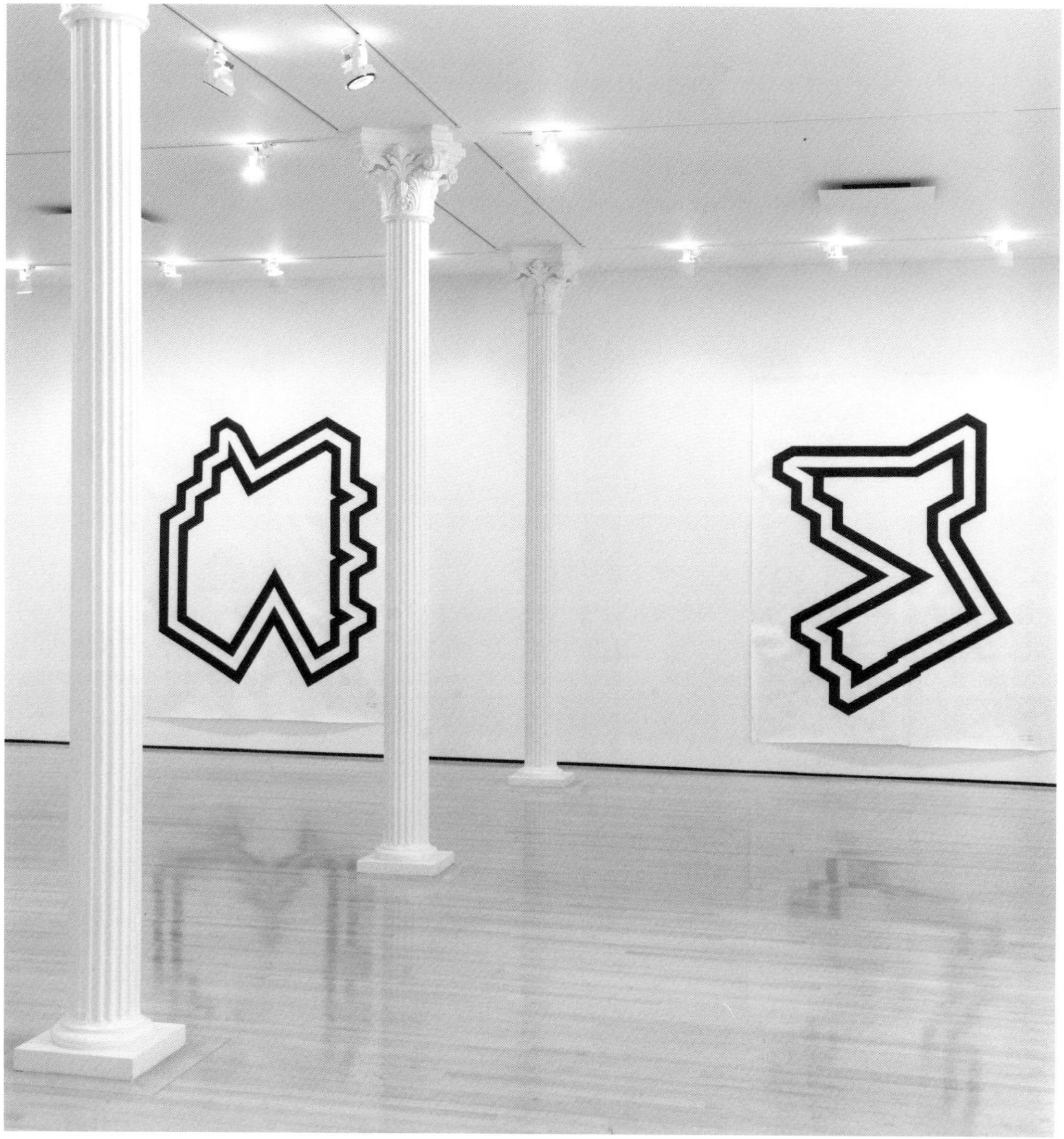

WORKS ON PAPER 1986 THE DRAWING CENTER, NYC

Reading a *Homeric Hymn to Aphrodite* in 1988, the artist was moved to invent a geometric figuration, using his hexagonal grid to generate forms. This research lasted ten years and included portraits, landscapes, and still-life paintings, in which the invention of abstract leaf shapes determined the course of his later paintings. This work was shown during a series of open-studio exhibitions, with his wife showing her ceramics, between 1990 and 1995, in the space they shared on Lafayette Street in SoHo.

While their new loft on West 38th Street was being remodeled, Federico and his wife spent time making work in their barn studio on a farm in upstate New York. In the spring of 1998, Federico made the first paintings with one large,

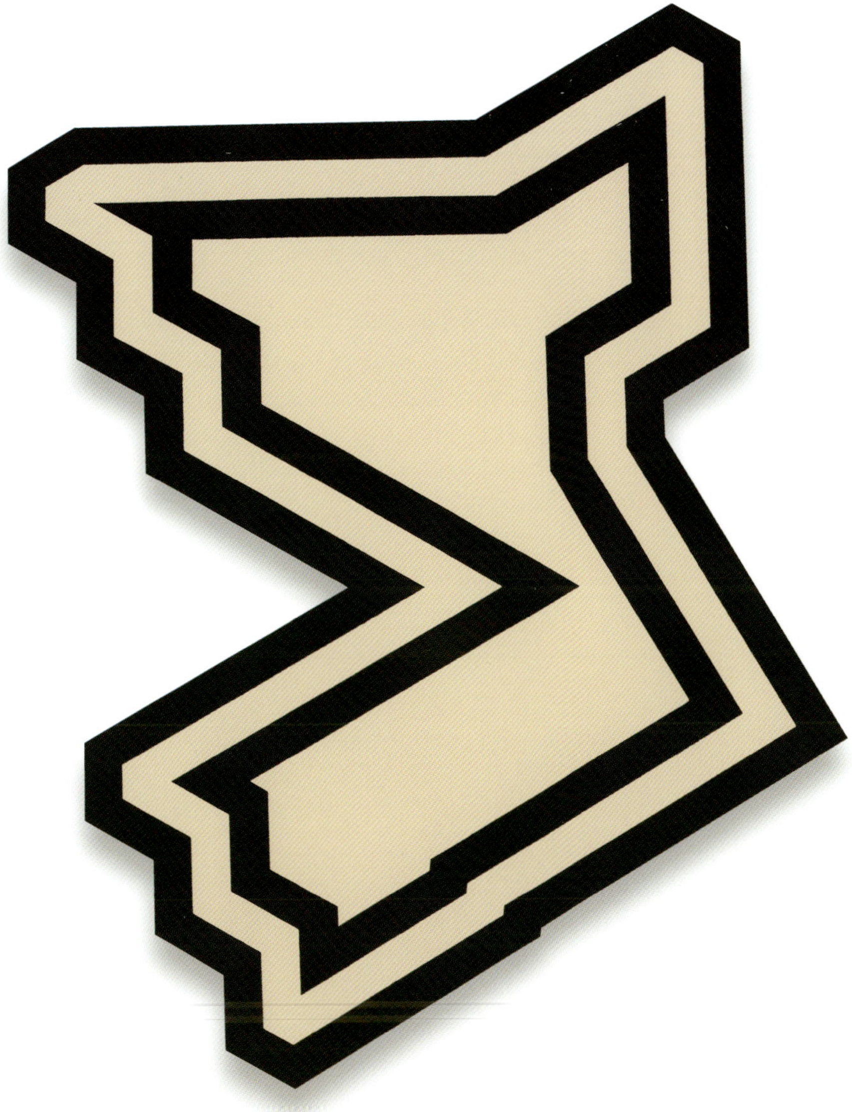

Dixie Chicken, 1986, 84" x 64", Acrylic on Shaped Canvas

stand-alone shape in a rectangle of pure color. Looking out at the countryside, "It was very, very quiet," Federico recalls. "Outside every window were these big, open, simple spaces. Suddenly, it was quite clear to me–a single shape can stand alone." This initiated a series that has continued for more than twenty years. These paintings unite his life long interests in movement (music, classical dance), gesture, plastic tension, pure color, and subtle, seemingly handless facture. The result is lively, bold, and immaculate configurations, with the graphic power of letter forms, logos, and heraldry. In this series, Federico's life's work has been realized. The work has been shown extensively in a number of solo shows in recent years.

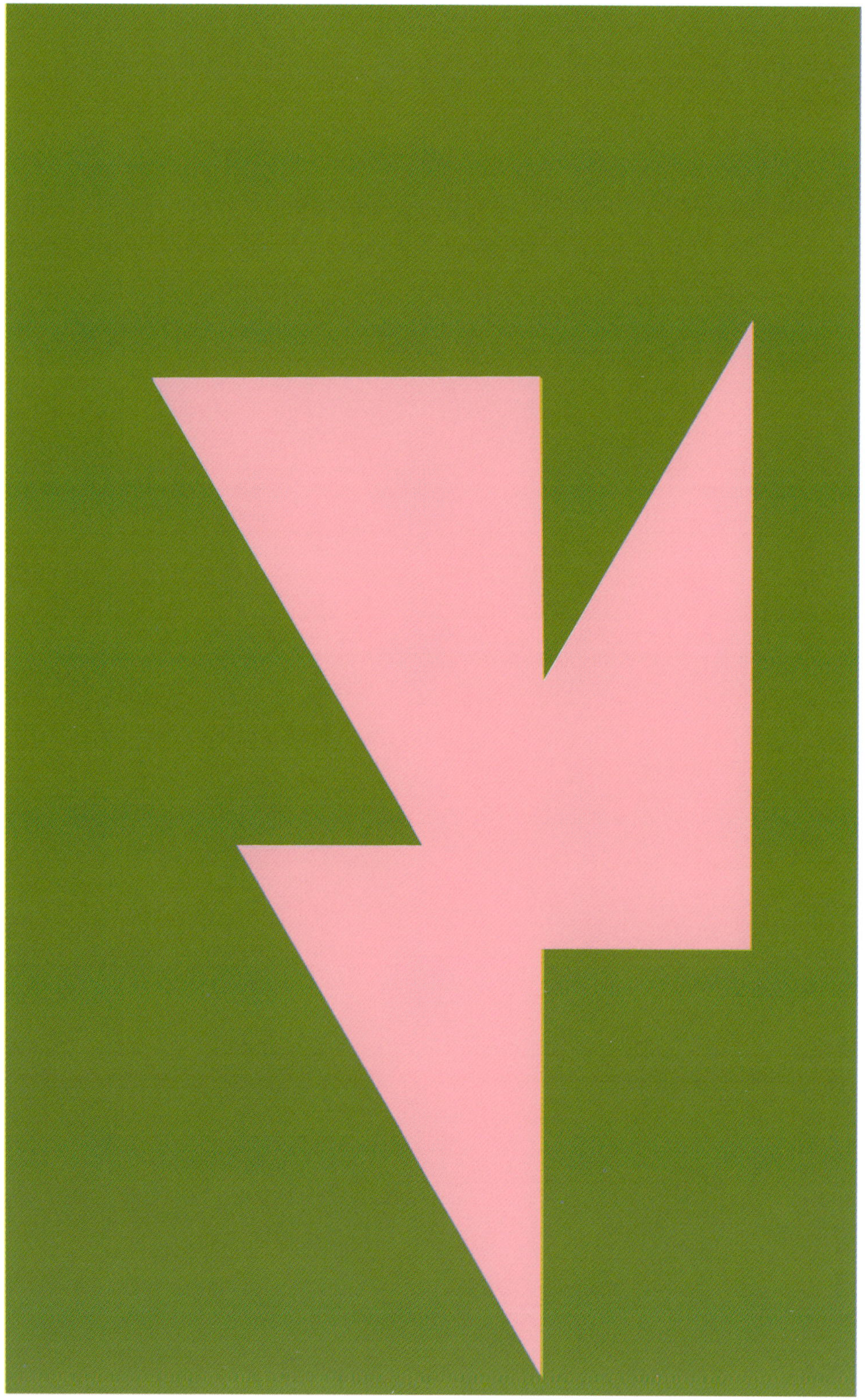

Barnabas, 1998, 34 1/4" x 20 7/8", Oil on Canvas

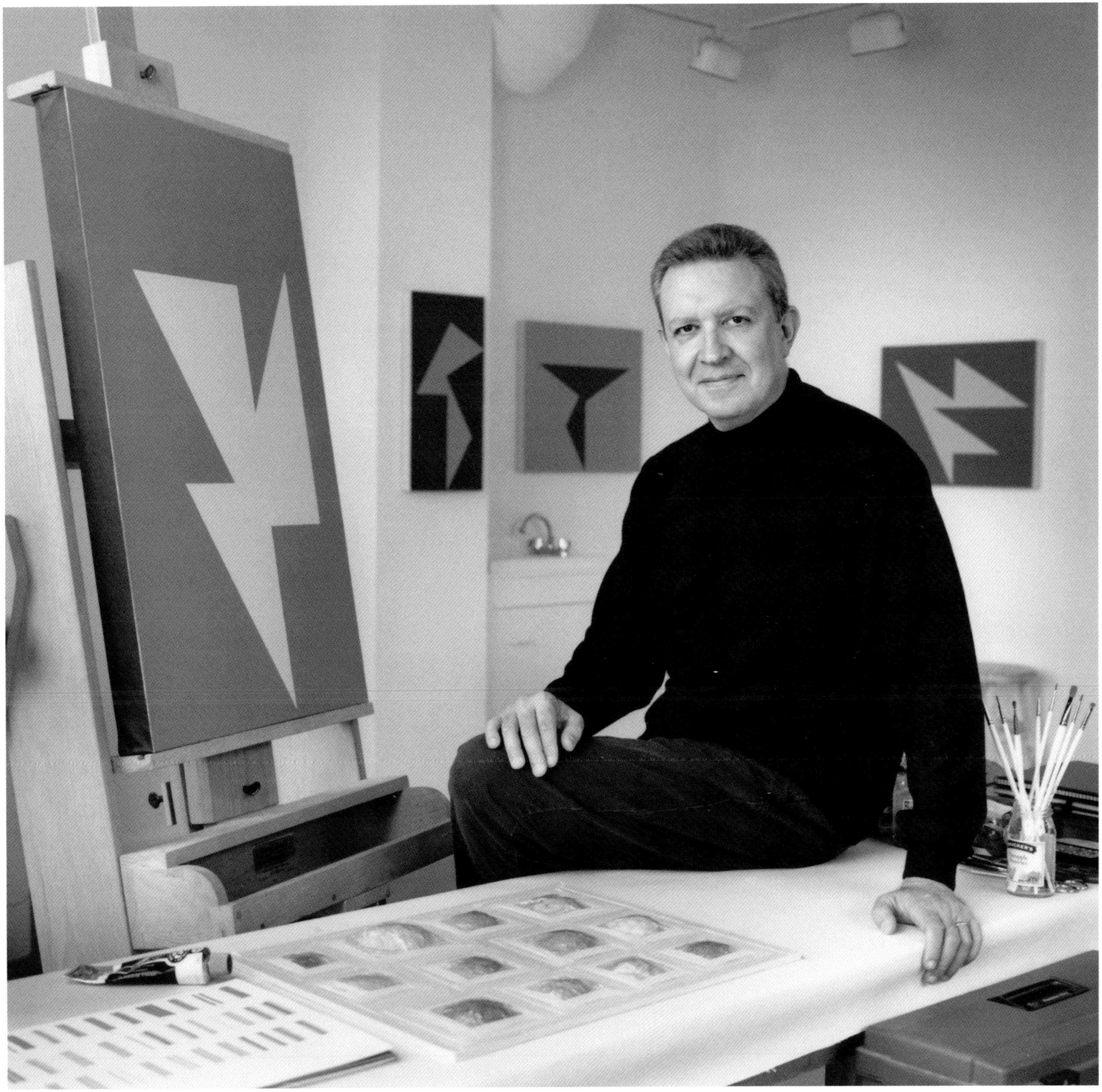

SALVATORE FEDERICO, 1999, W 38 ST STUDIO, NYC

Salvatore Federico Paintings: Early Works

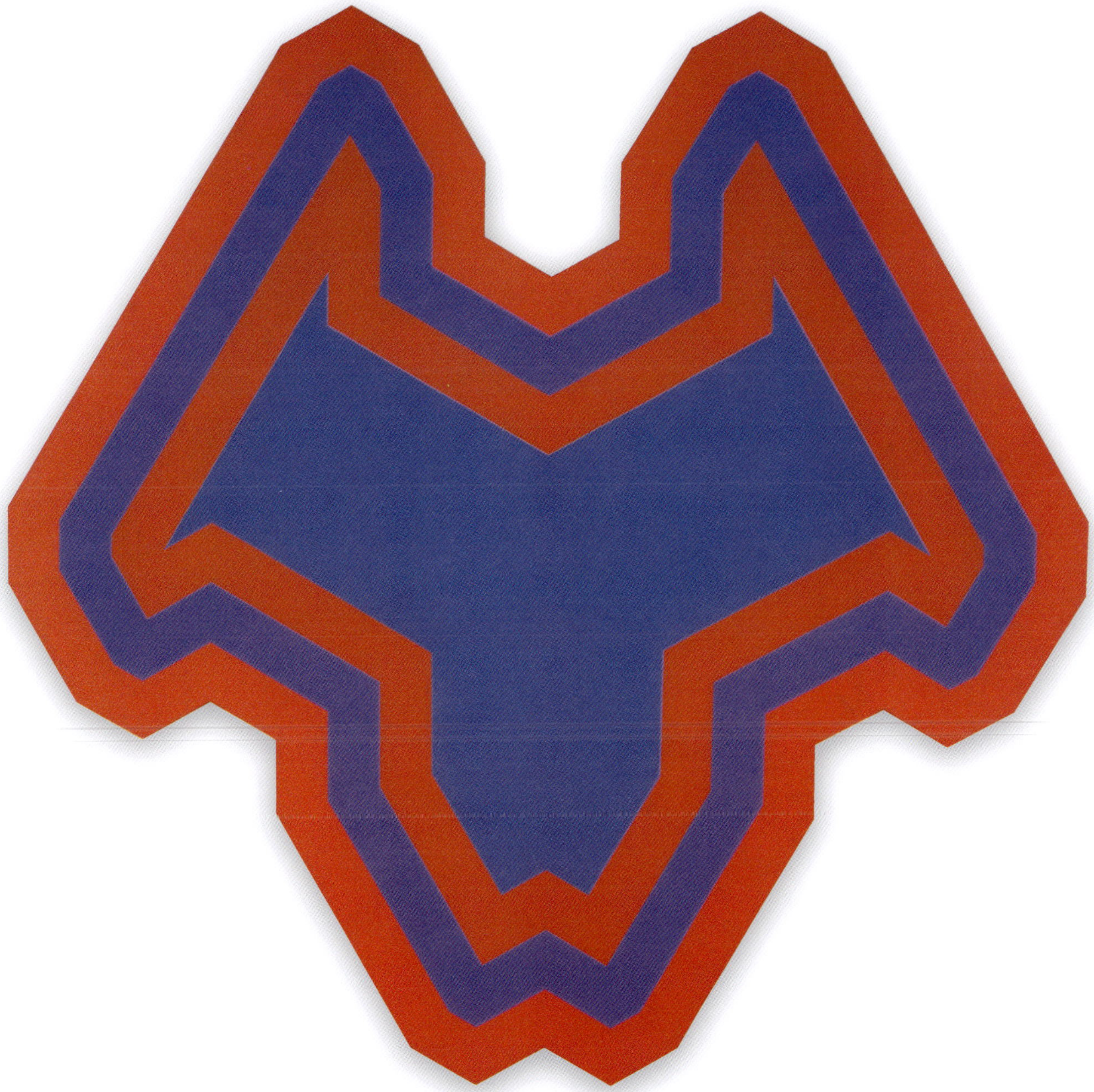

Spirit, 1968, 84" x 84", Acrylic on Shaped Canvas

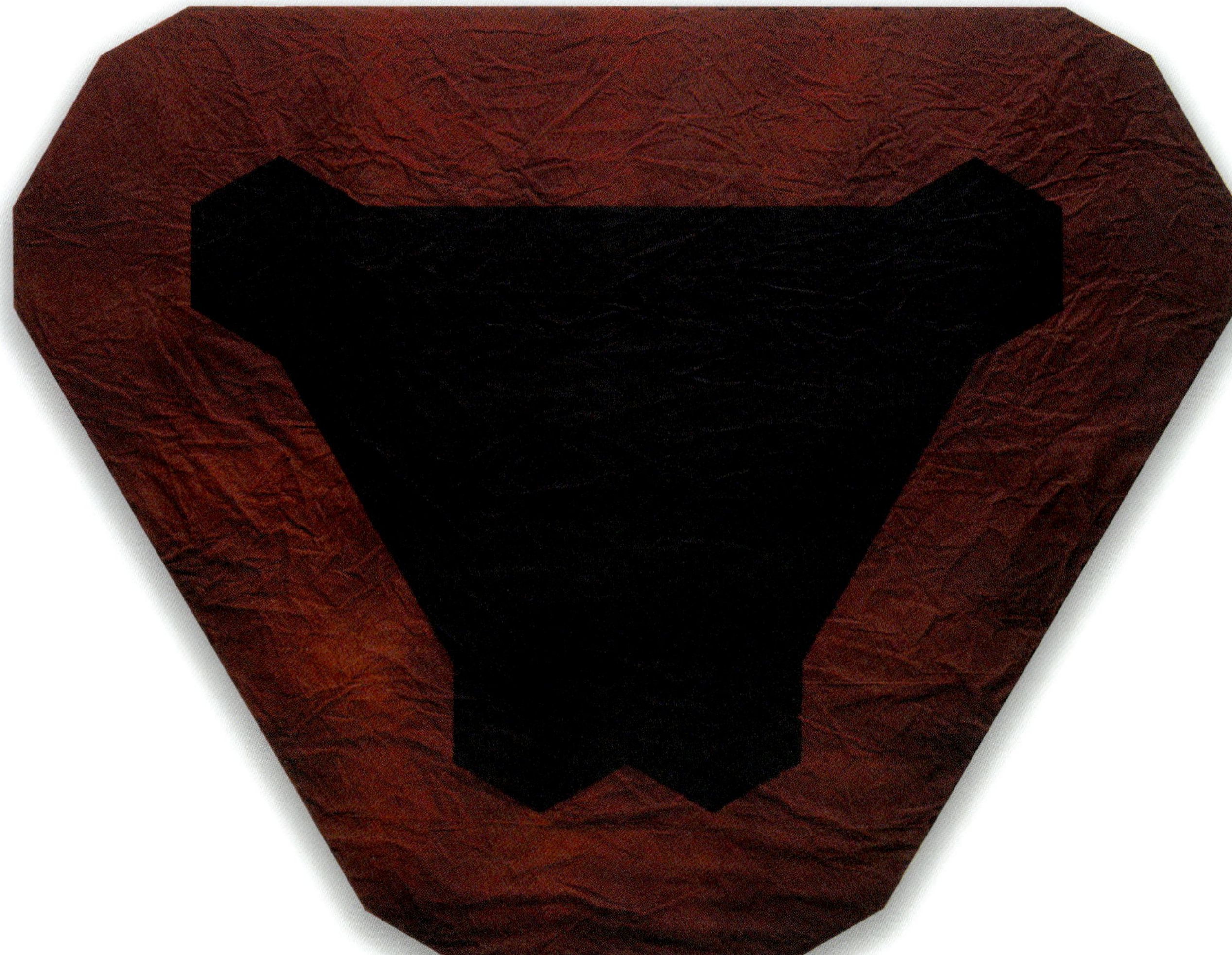

Liberation, 1970, 57 1/8" x 73 1/4", Acrylic on Shaped Canvas

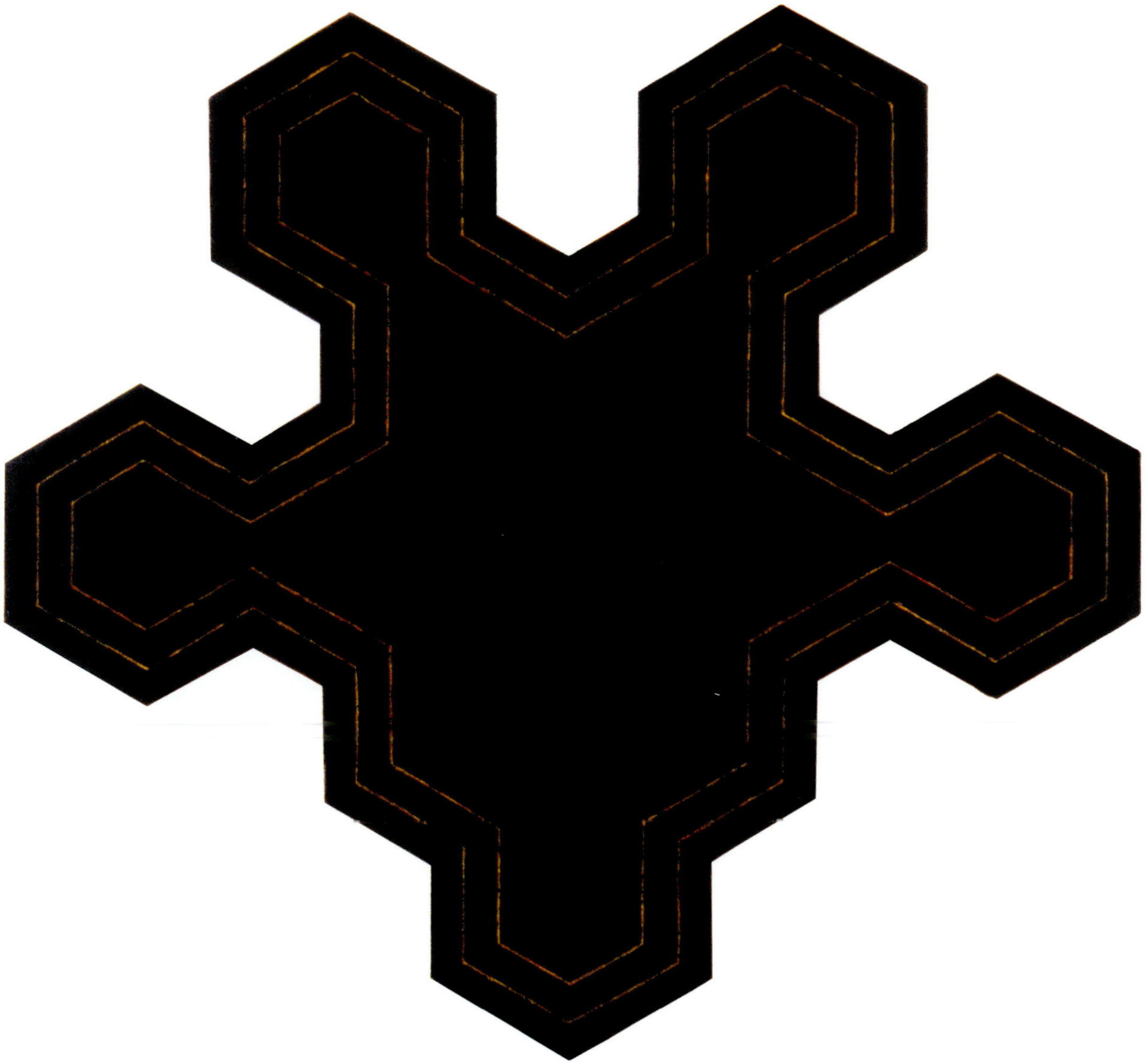

Headdress, 1971, 54" x 60", Acrylic on Shaped Canvas
Private Collection, NJ

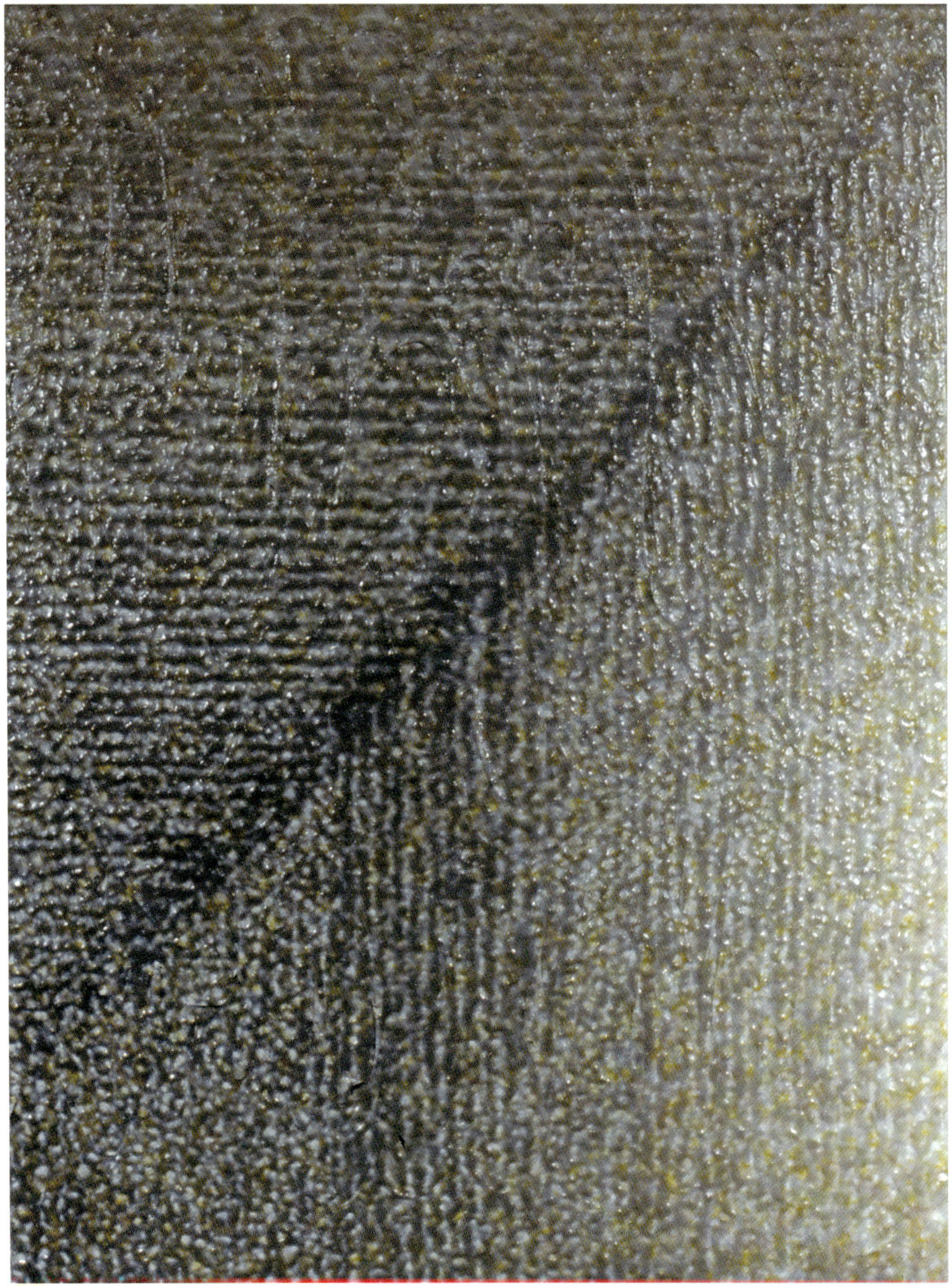

12-12-1978, 60" x 48", Acrylic on Canvas

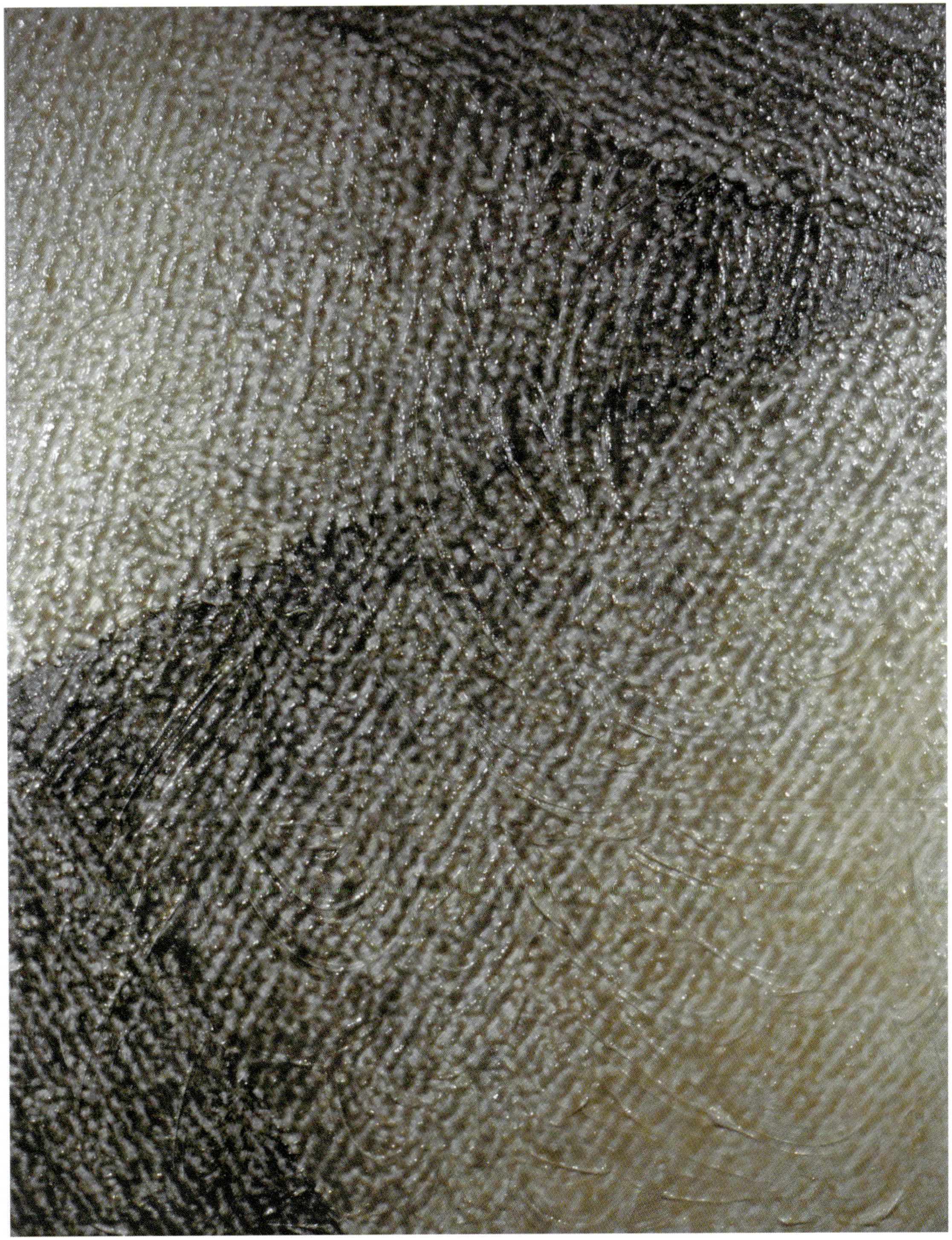

06-23-1980, 66" x 50", Acrylic on Canvas

PASSAGE, 1981, 44" x 60", Acrylic on Canvas

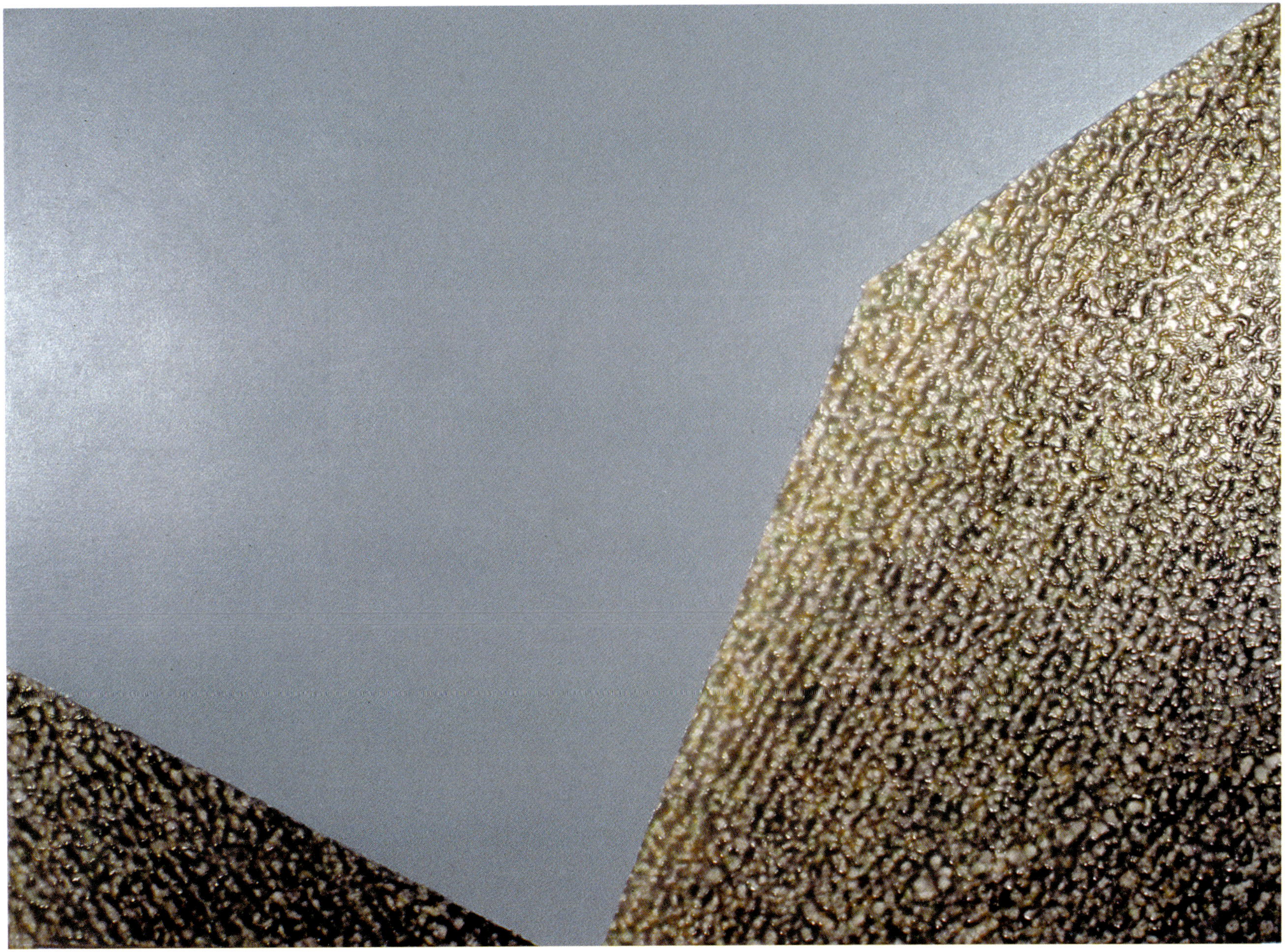

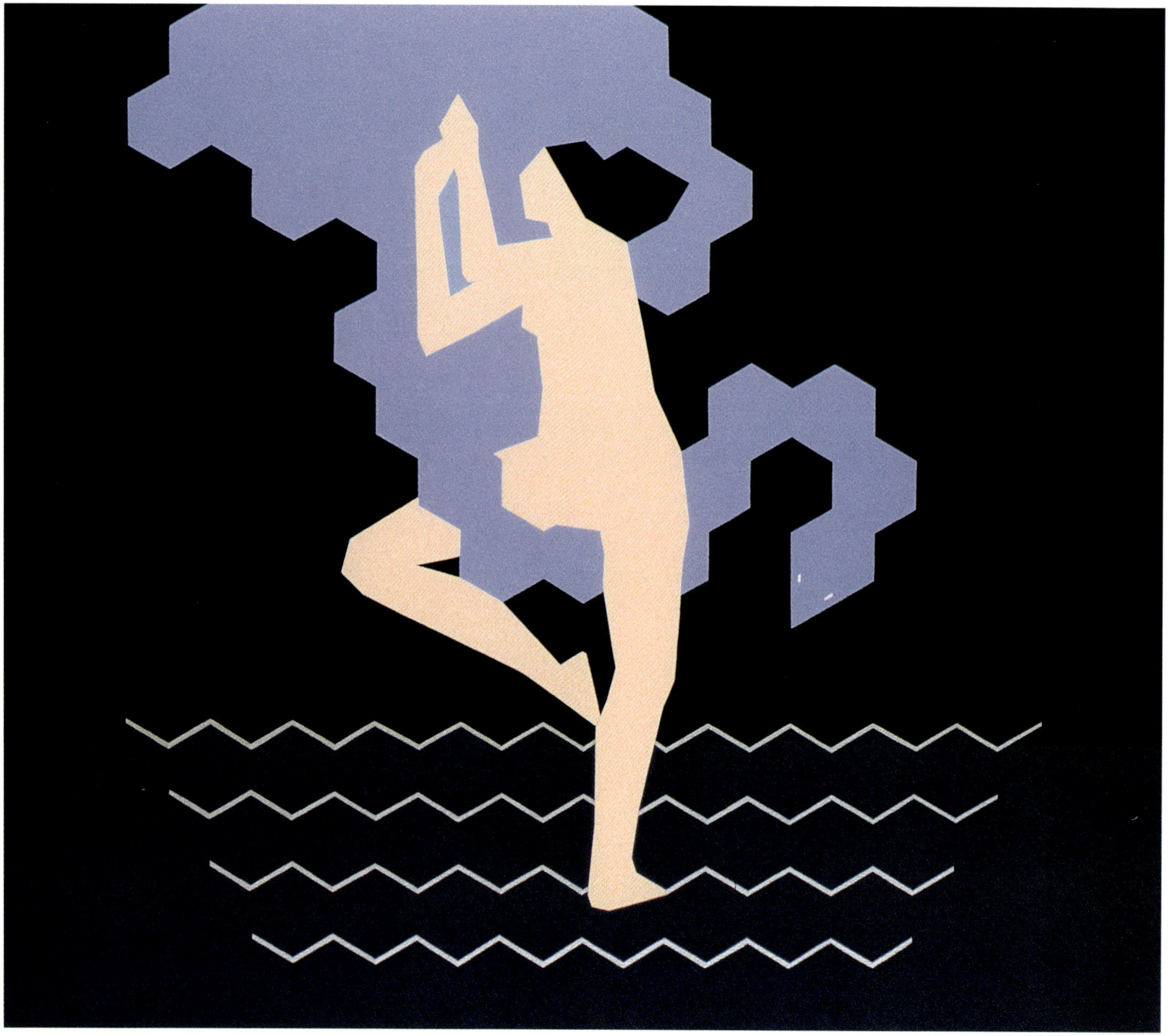

Eurynome, 1989, 52 1/2" x 59 1/2", Acrylic on Canvas

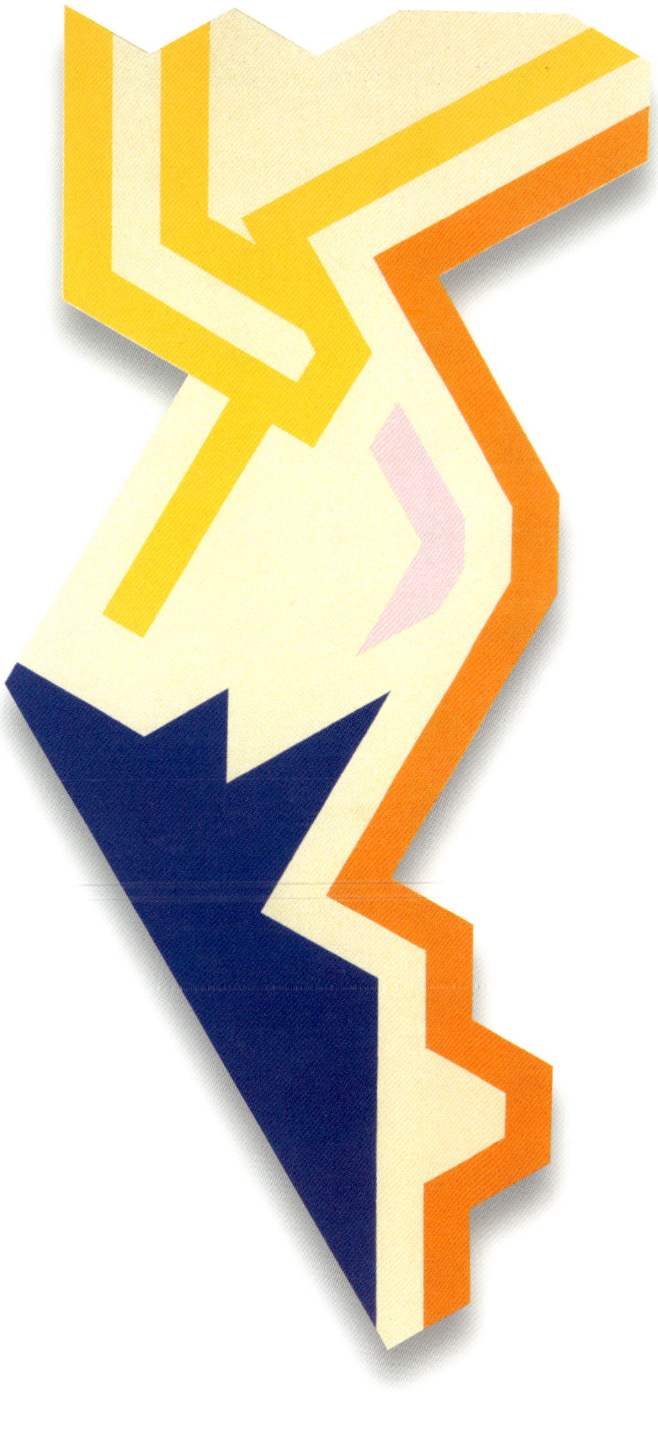

Anchises, 1988, 84" x 42", Acrylic on Shaped Canvas

Lafayette Street, 1994, 55 7/8" x 42 5/8", Oil on Canvas

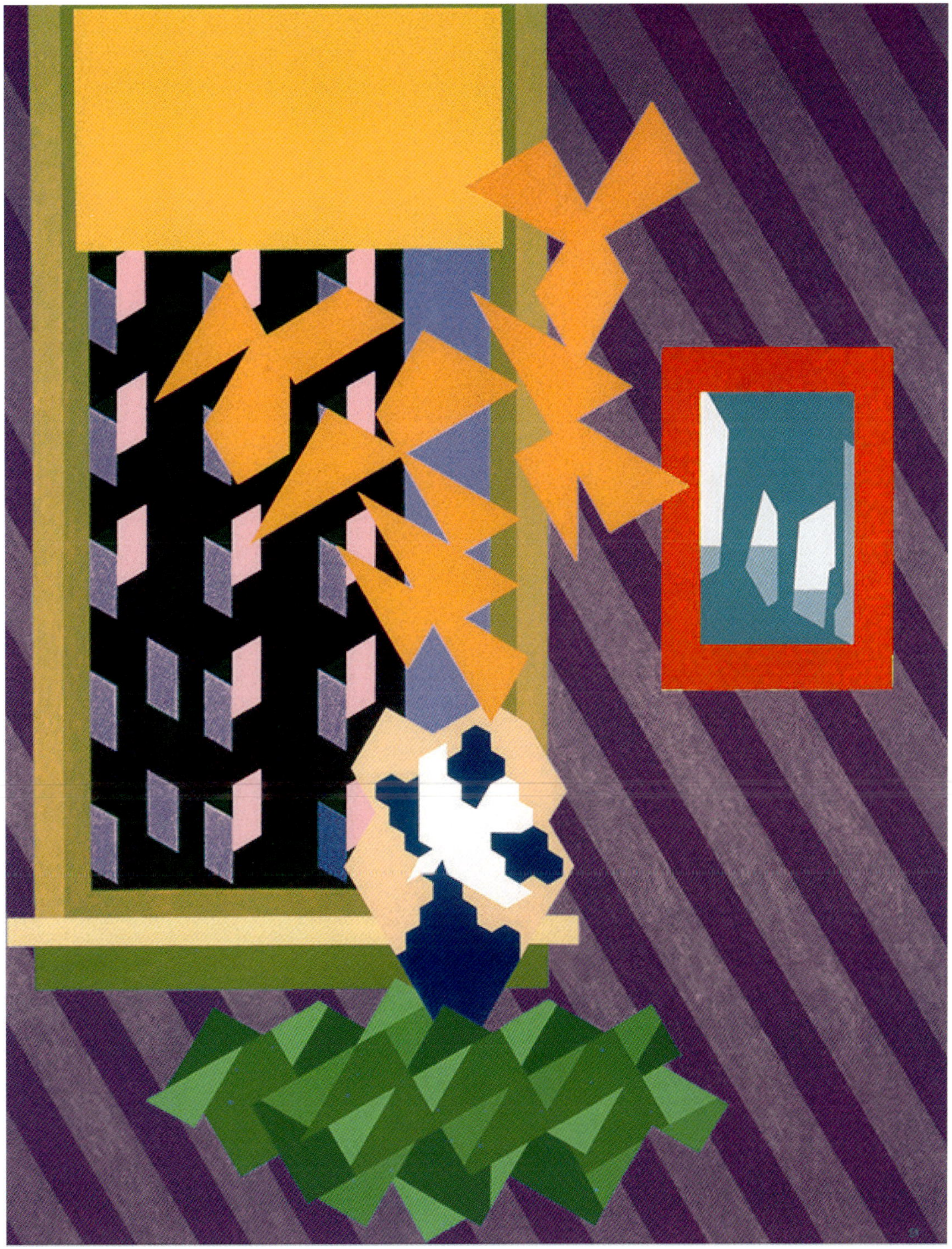

Salvatore Federico: Works 1998-2018

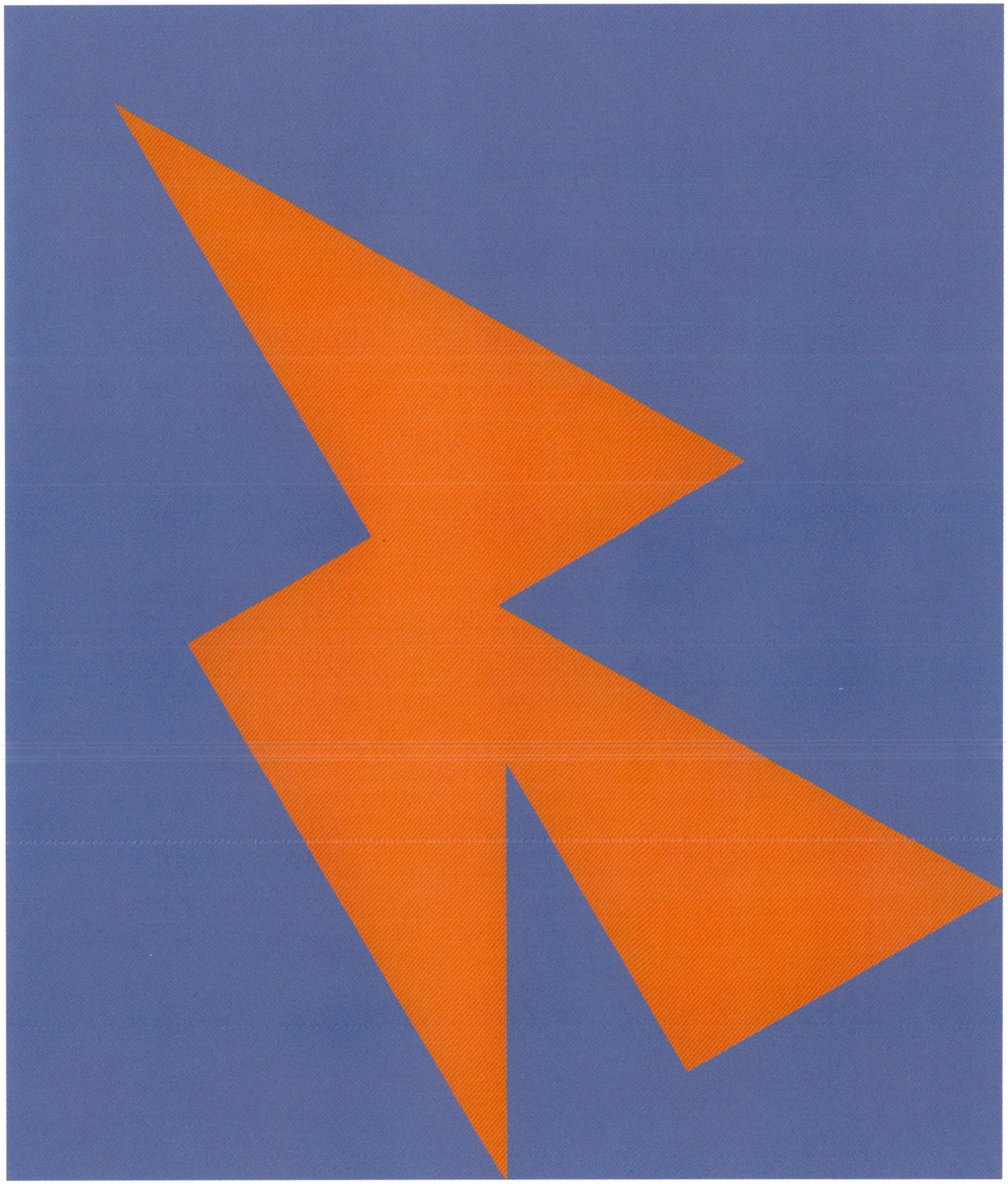

GERMANUS, 1998, 18 3/8" x 15 1/2", OIL ON CANVAS

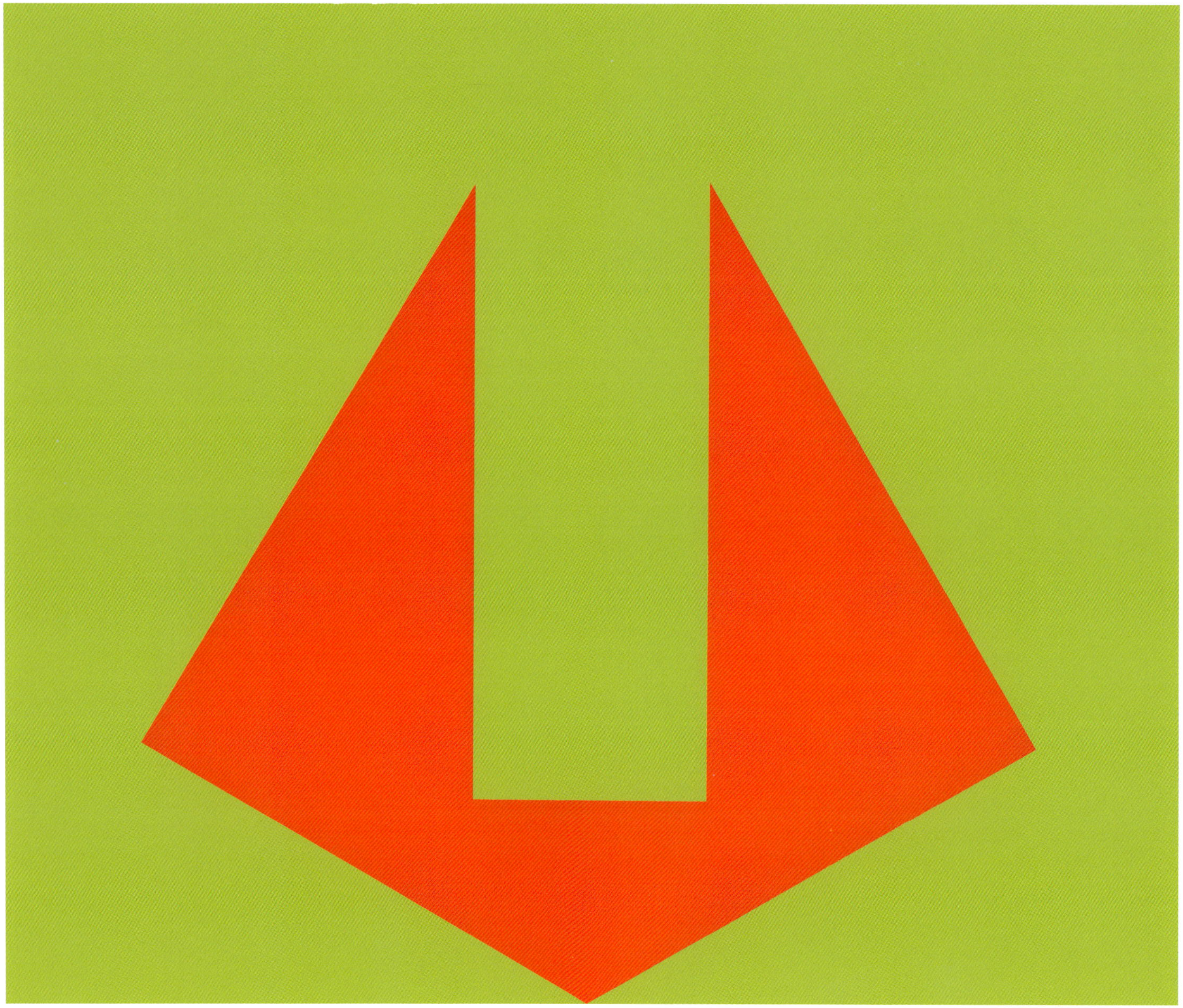

Theresa, 1998, 16 13/16" x 19 1/2", Oil on Canvas

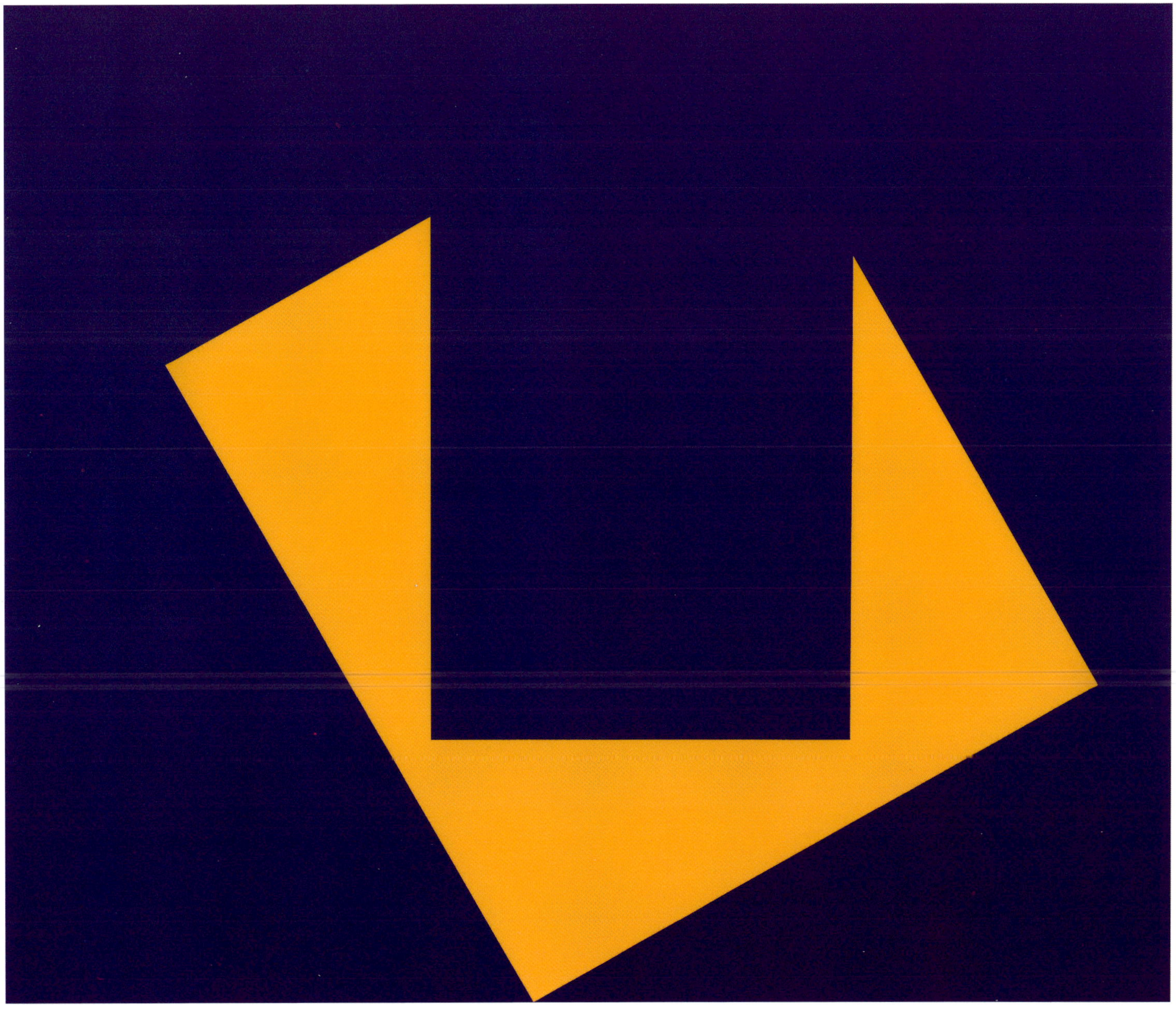

Remi, 1998, 18 3/8" x 21 1/2", Acrylic on Canvas

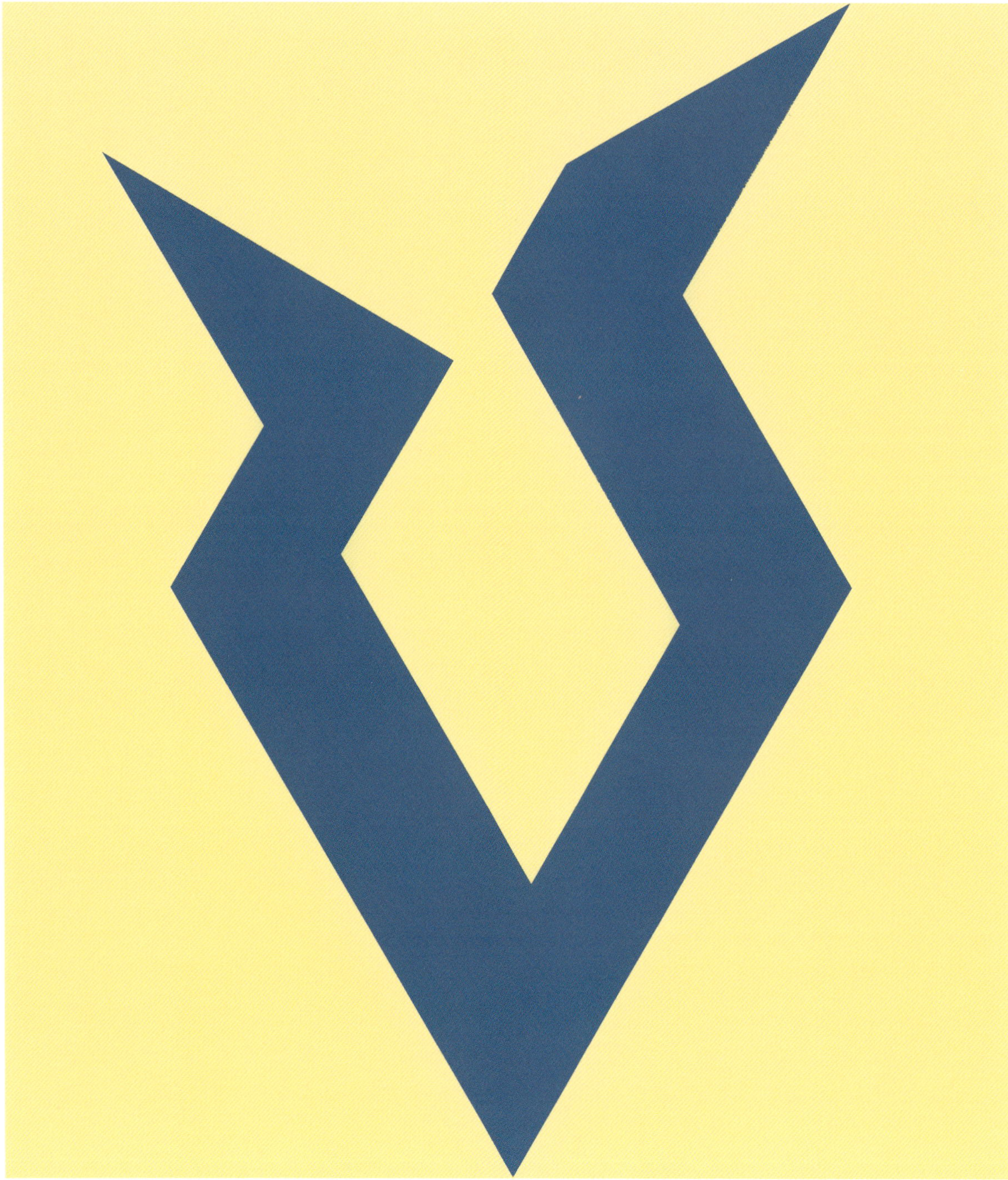

Francesca, 1999, 21 15/16" x 19", Oil on Canvas

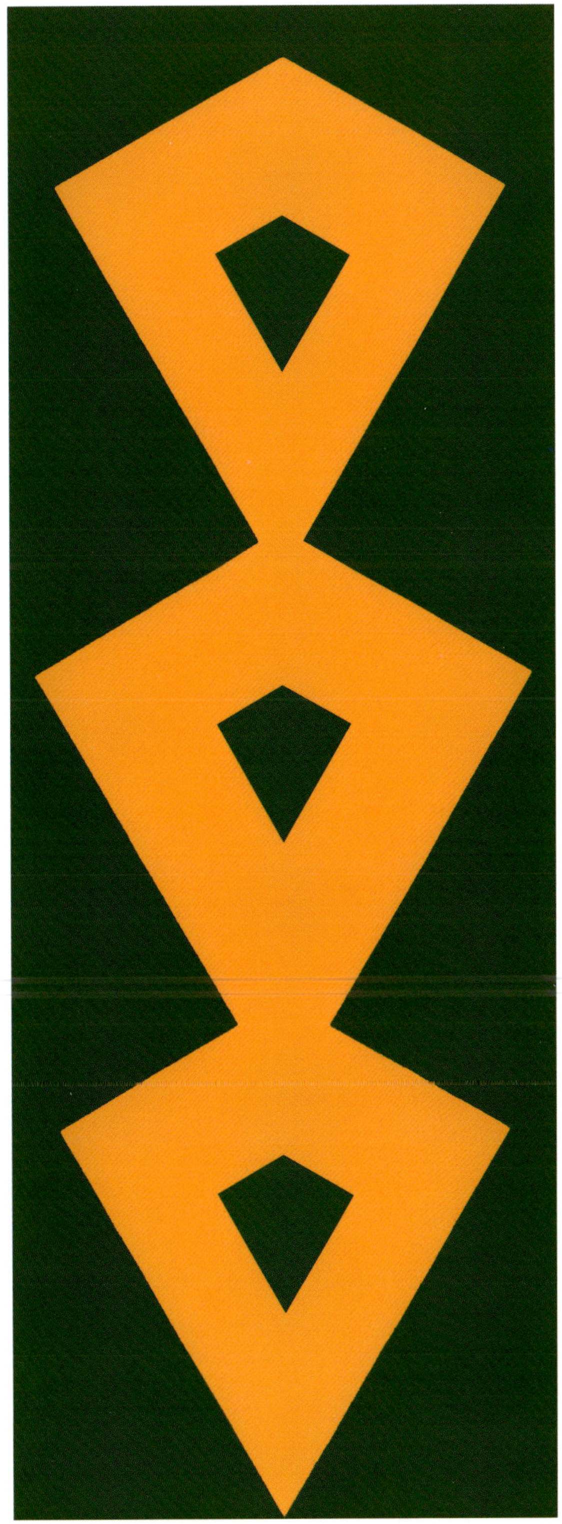

Constantine, 1999, 35 3/8" x 12 11/16", Oil on Canvas

Kateri, 1999, 24 3/4" x 28 7/8", Acrylic on Canvas

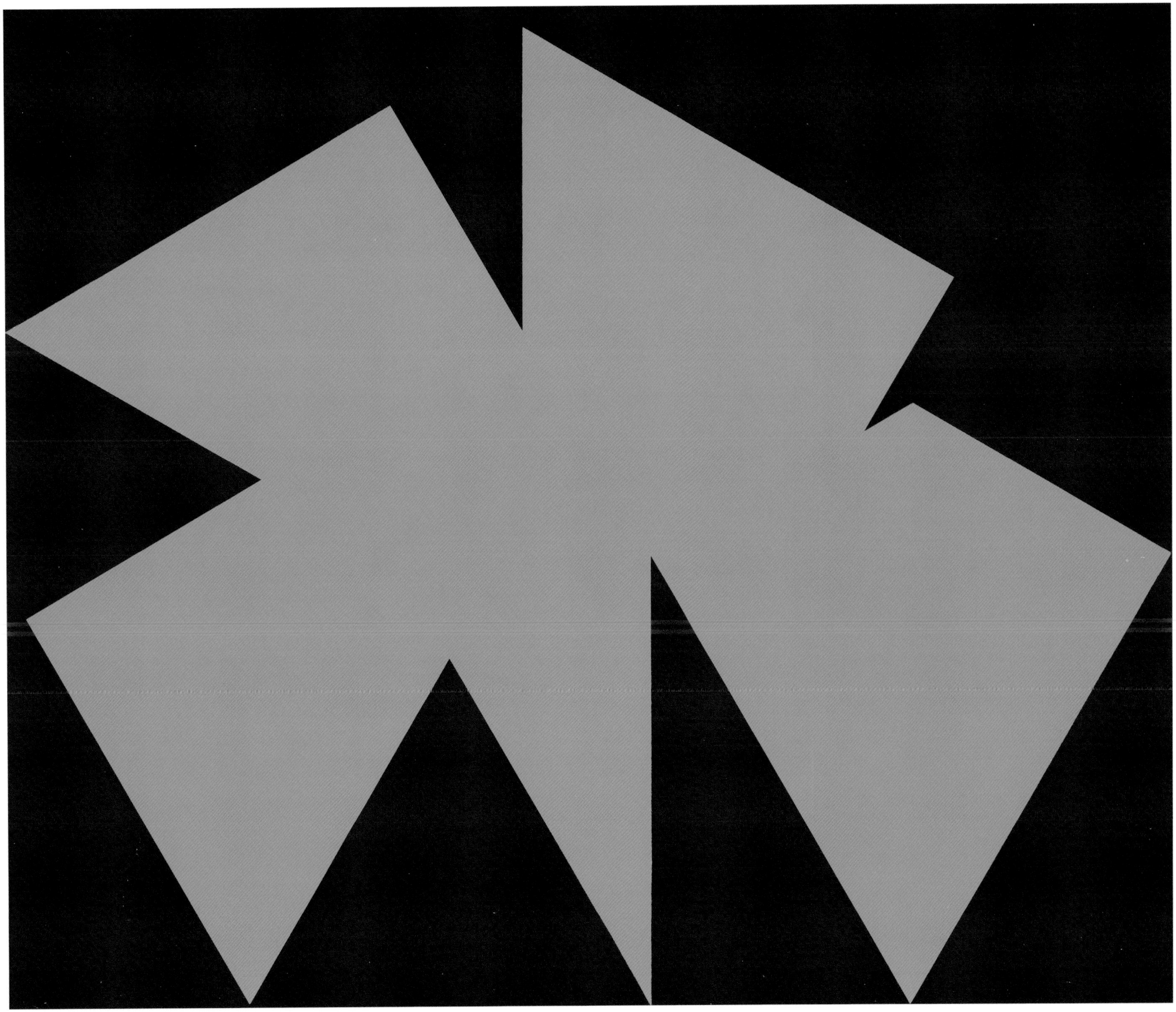

Celestine V, 1999, 18 5/8" x 26 1/8", Oil on Canvas

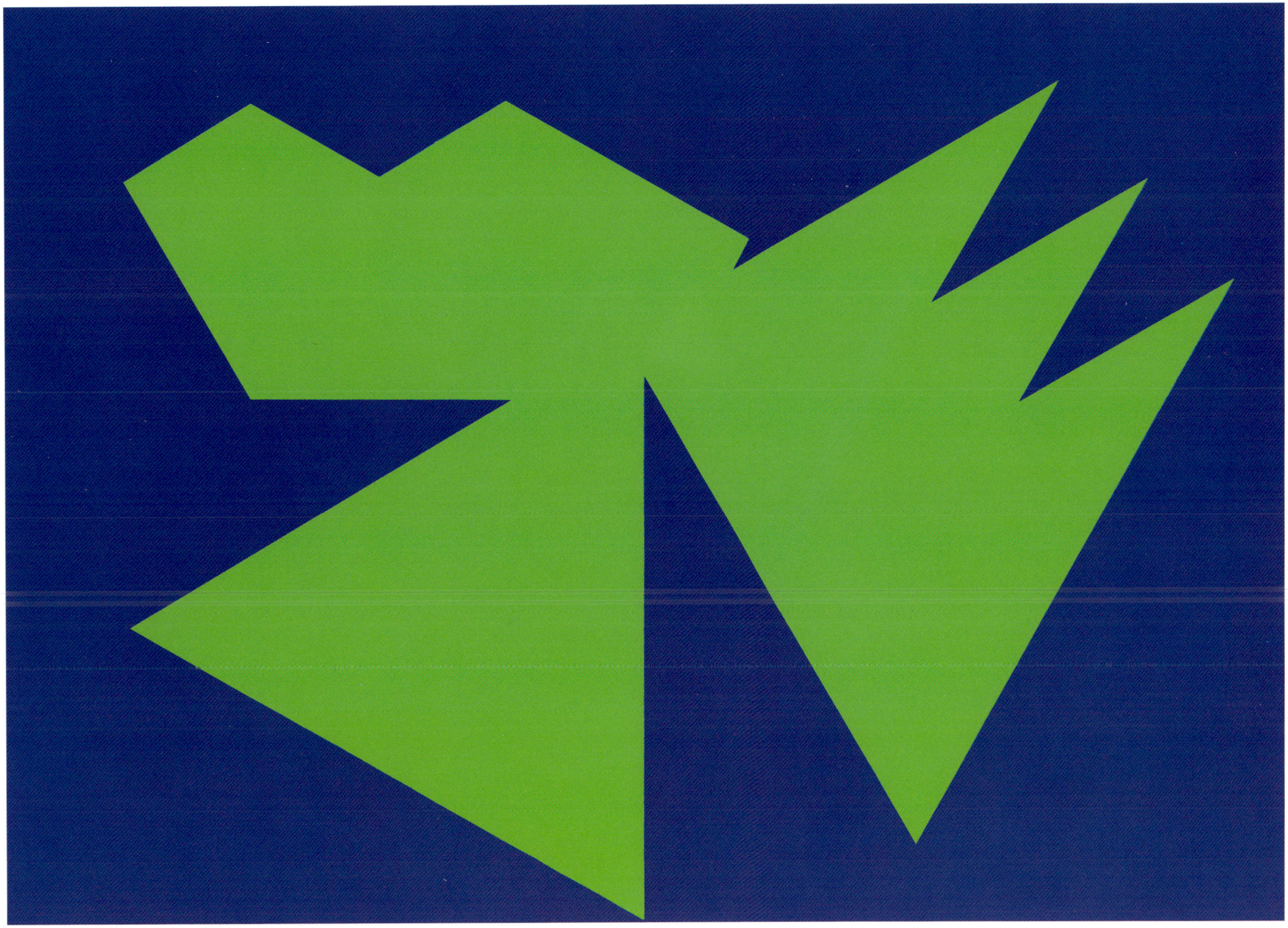

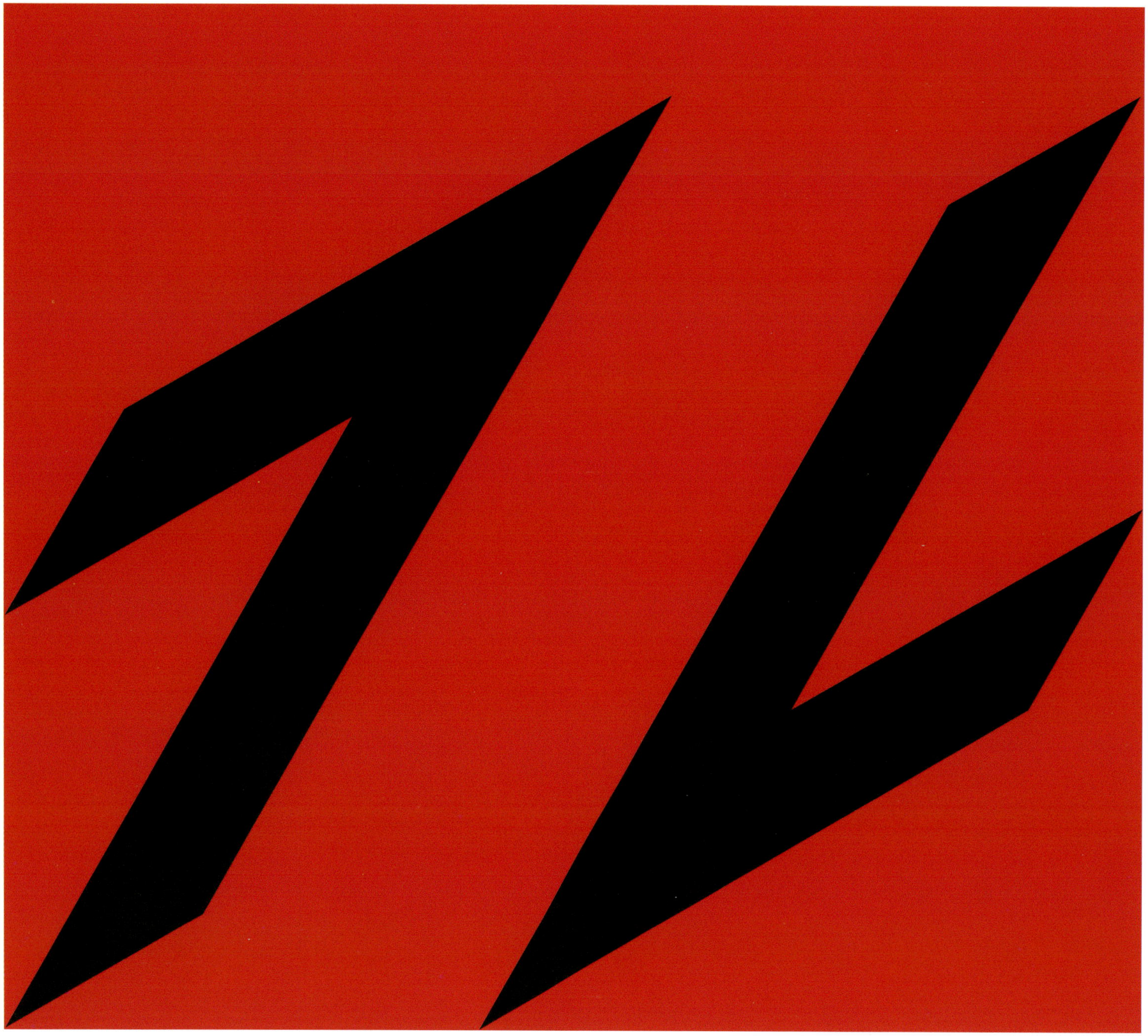

Arcadius, 2000, 23" x 25 1/2", Oil on Canvas

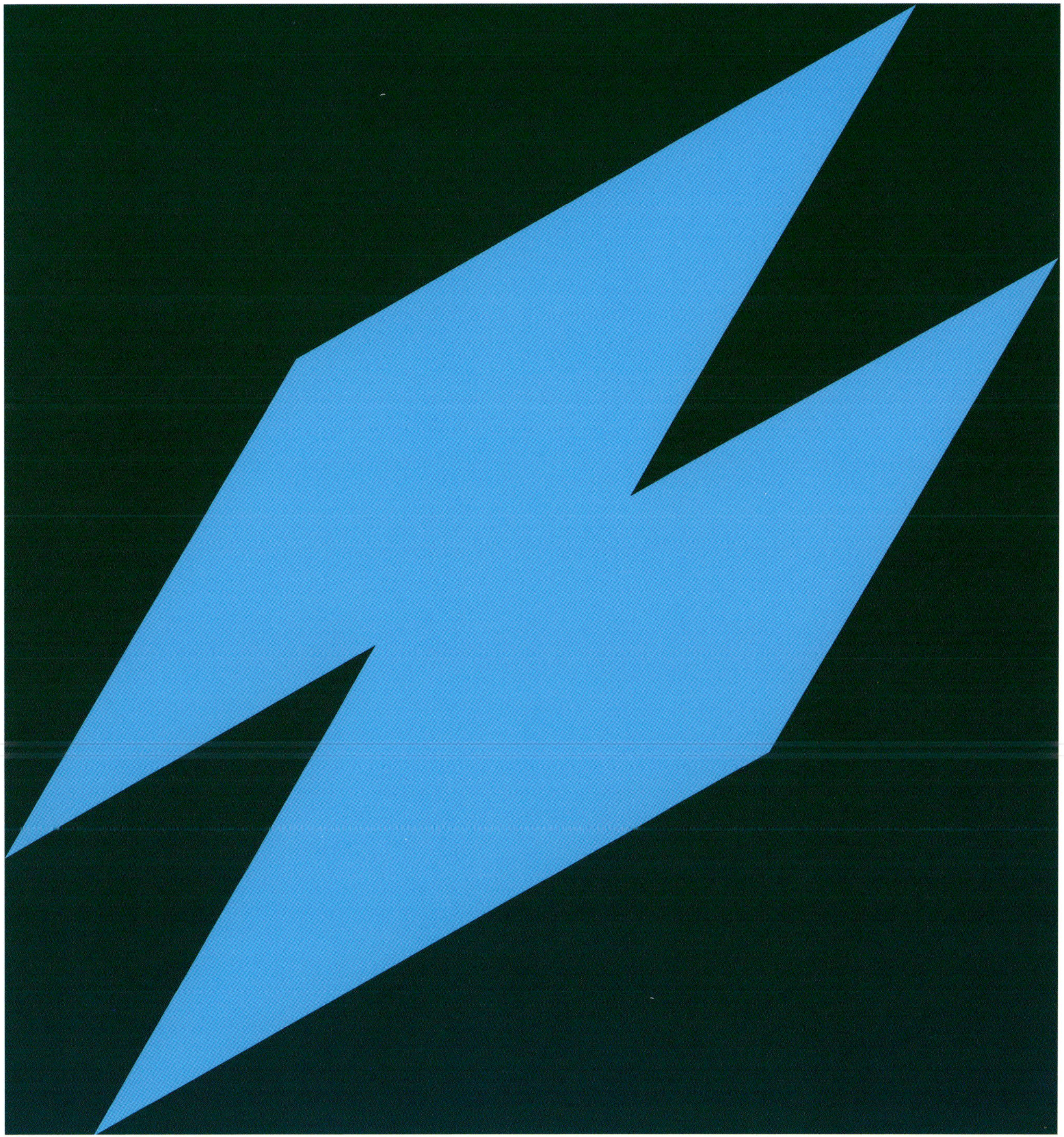

Hilary of Poitiers, 2000, 20 13/16" x 19 3/16", Acrylic on Canvas

Woolo, 2001, 21 5/16" x 38 1/16", Acrylic on Canvas

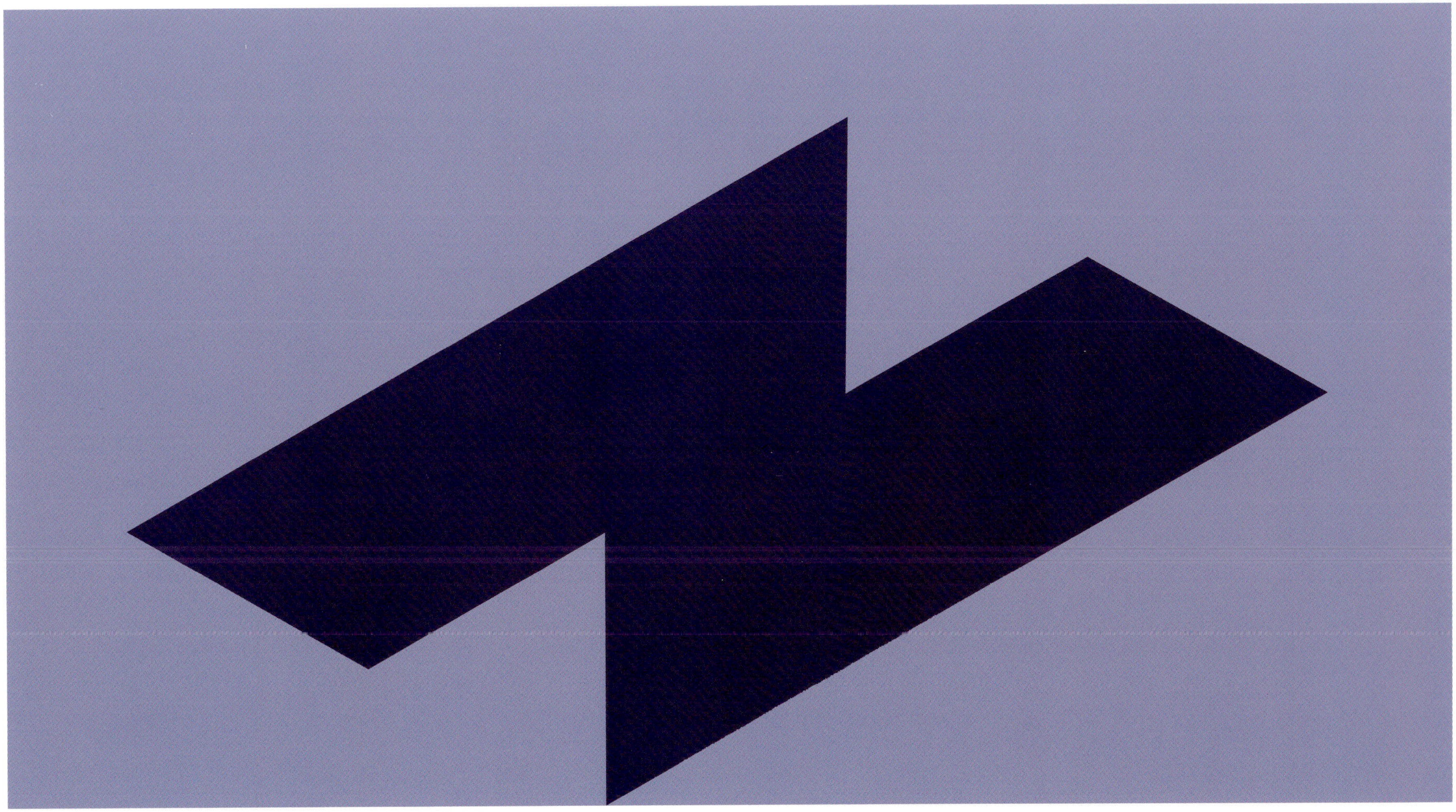

Baptism, 2002, 79 3/4" x 80 1/2", Acrylic on Canvas

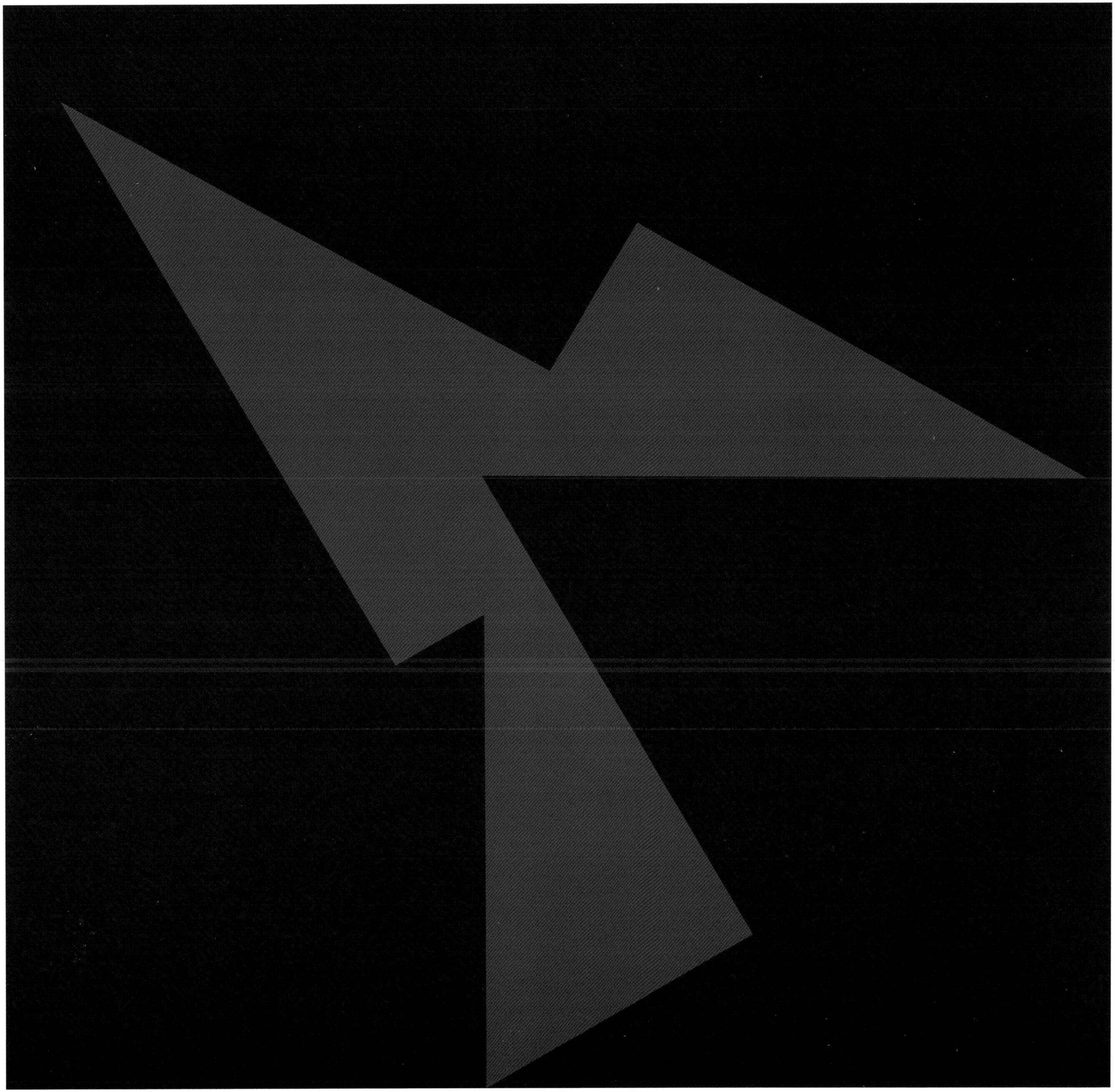

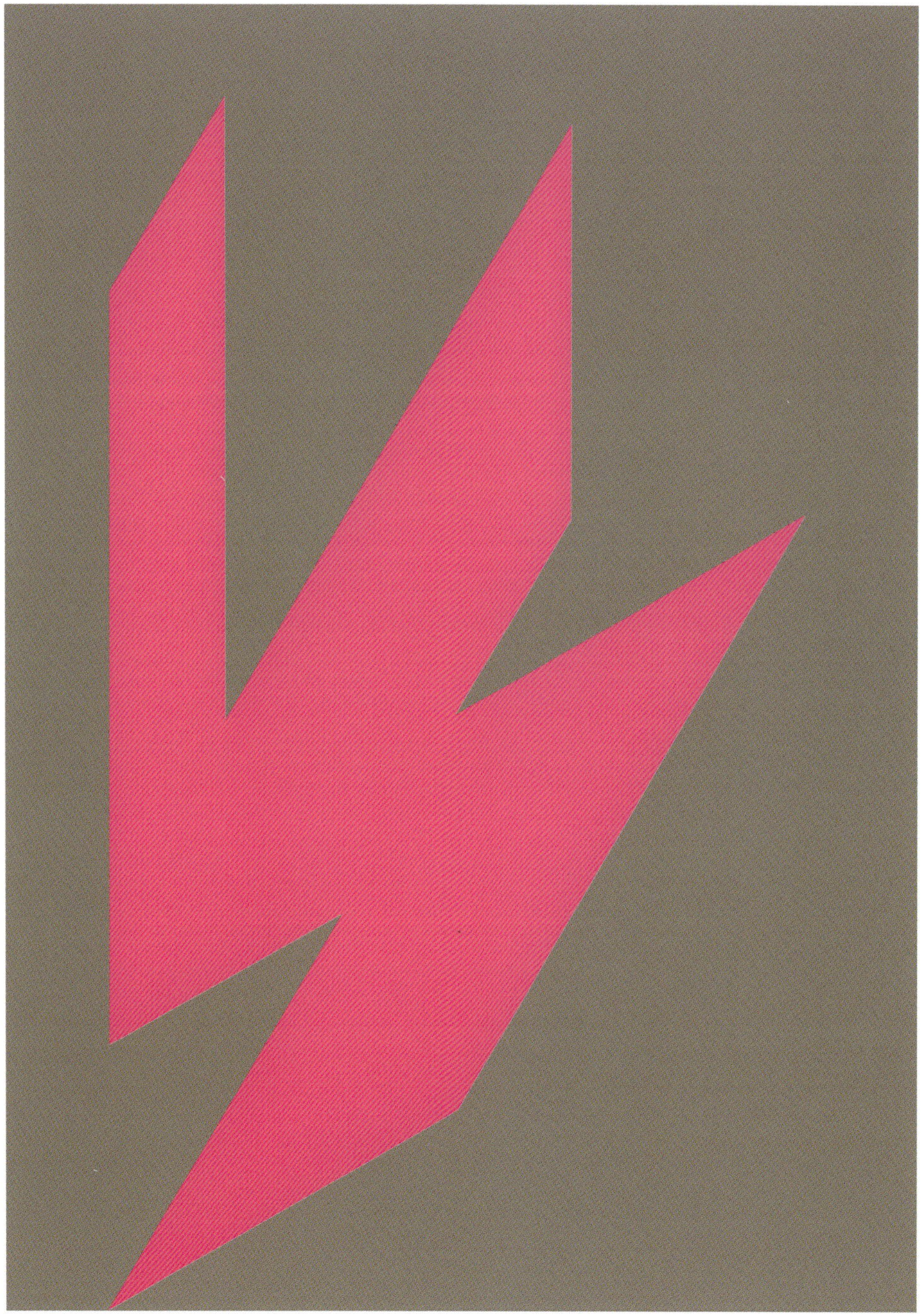

VALÈRY, 2001, 35 7/8" x 25 3/8", ACRYLIC ON CANVAS

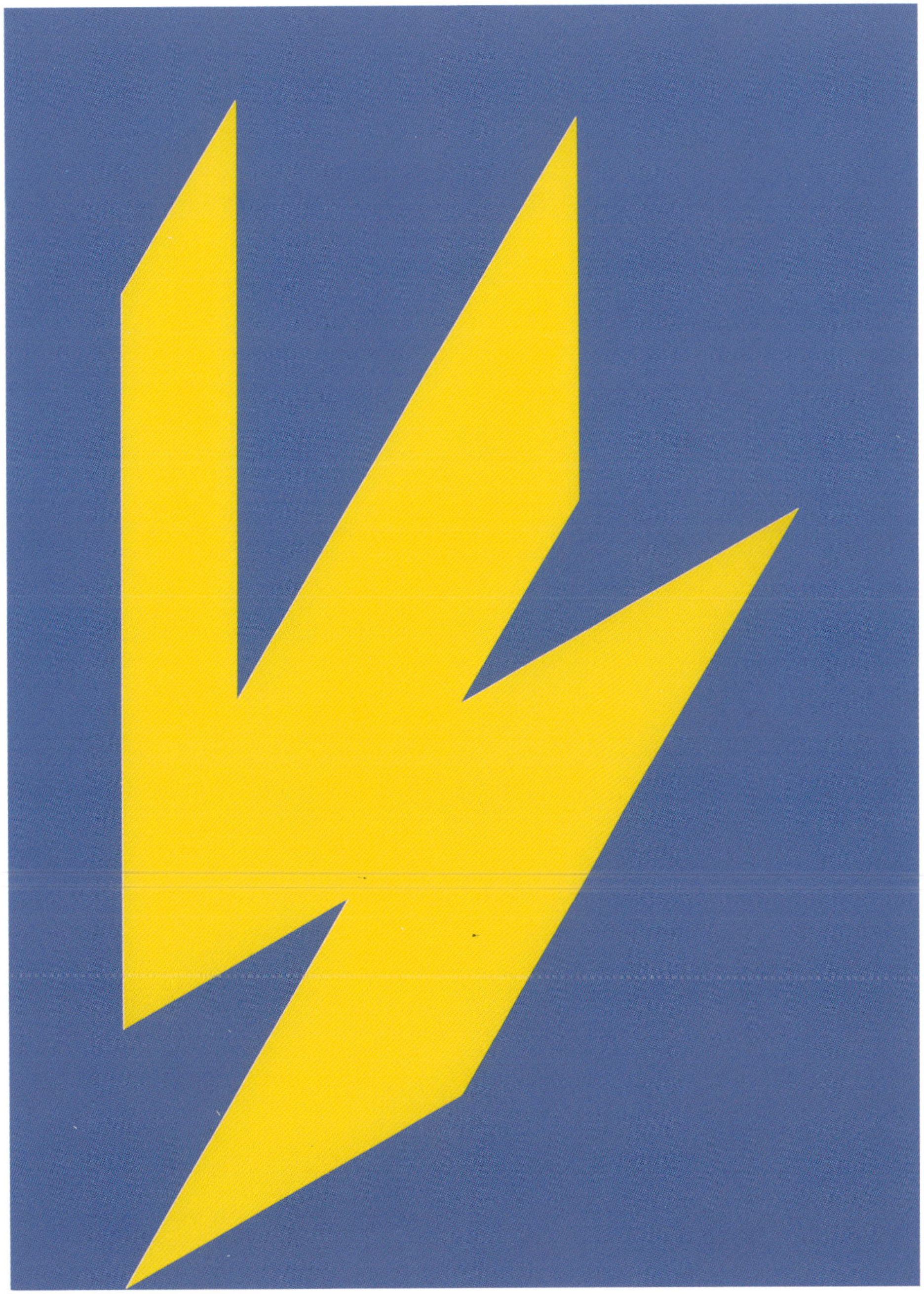

Valèry 2, 2001-07, 36 5/8" x 25 3/4", Acrylic on Canvas

D'ADDIO, 2002, 71 3/8" x 67 7/8", Acrylic on Canvas

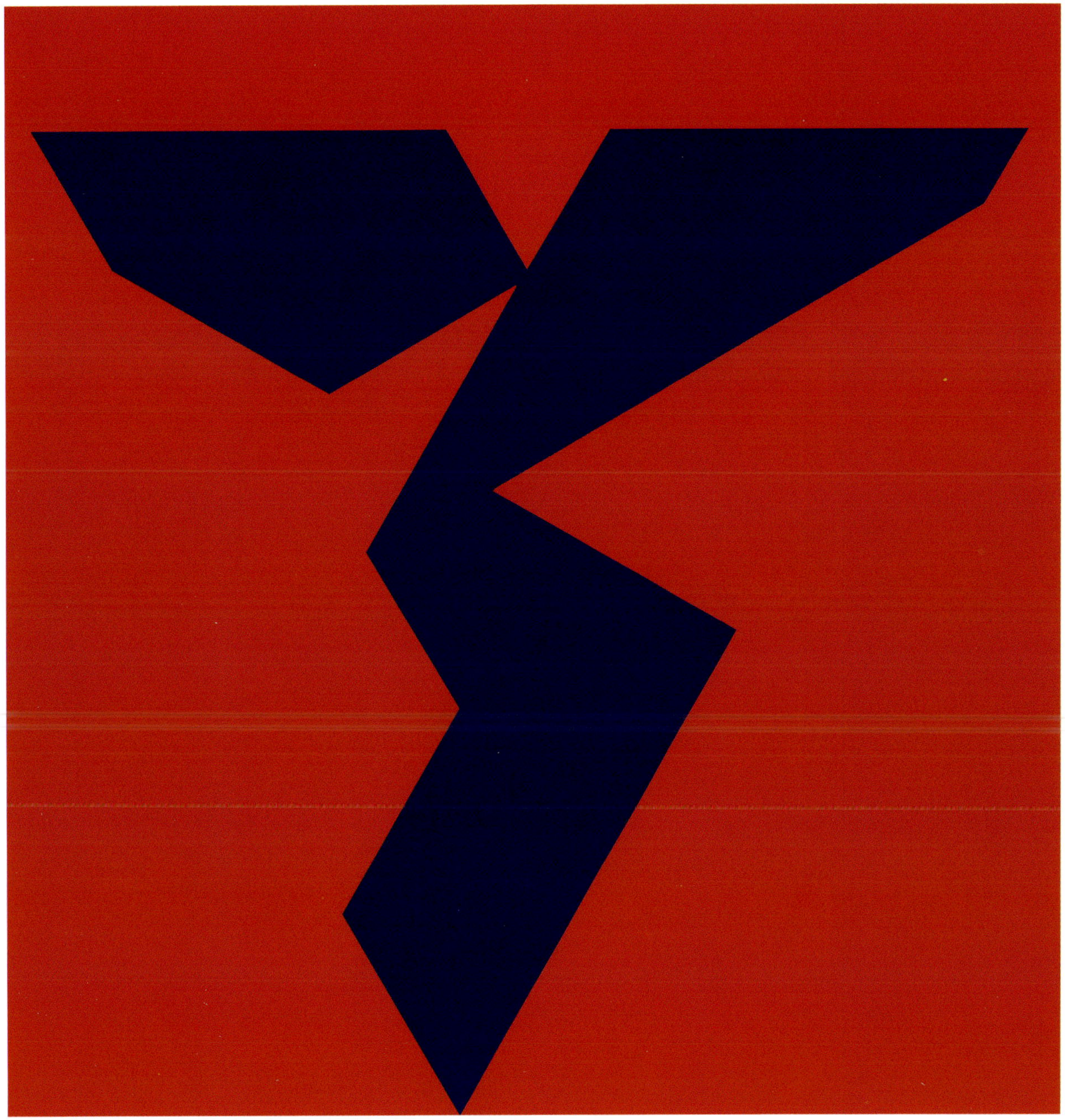

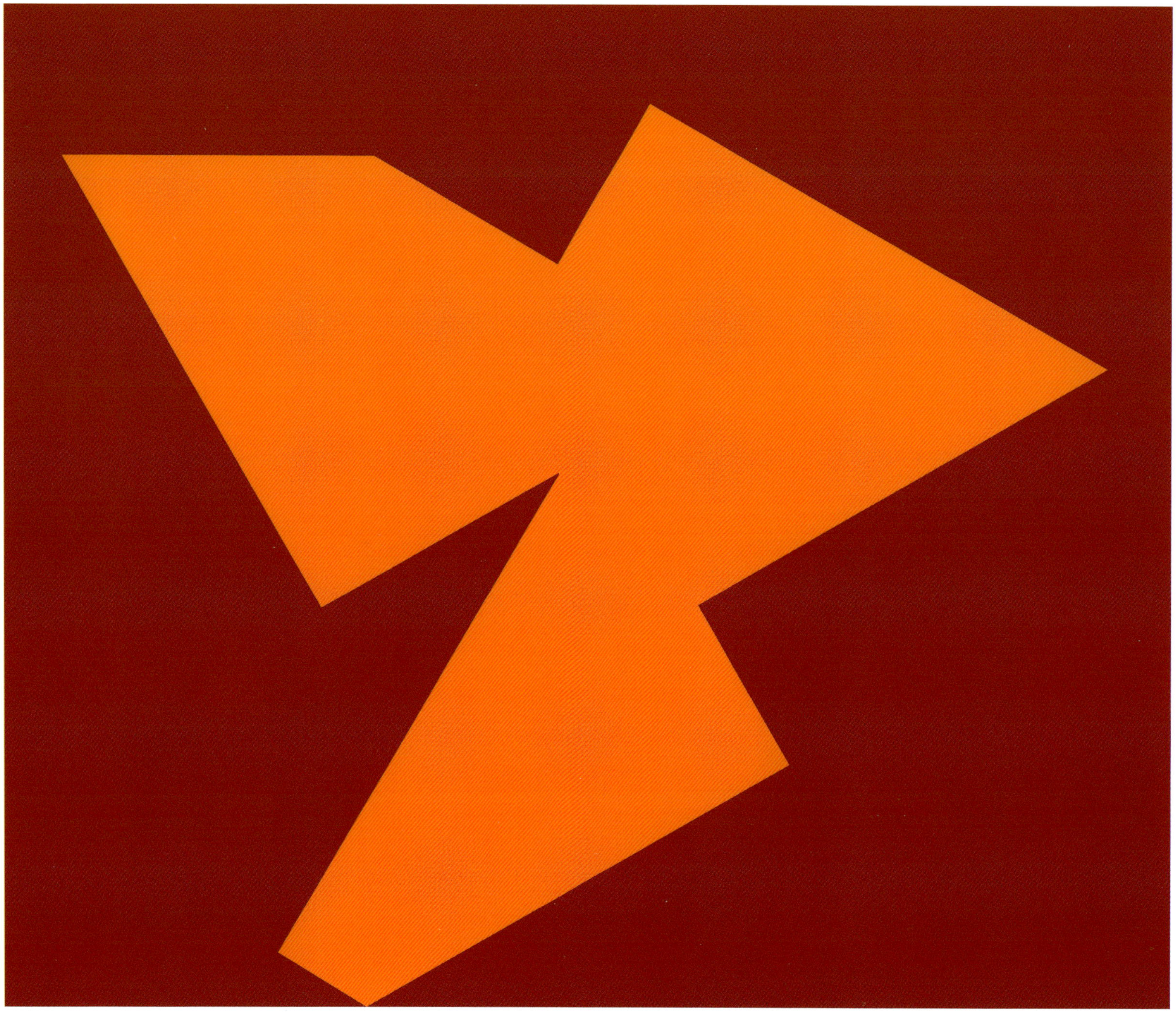

EUTYCHIUS, 2002, 52 3/4" x 61", Acrylic on Canvas

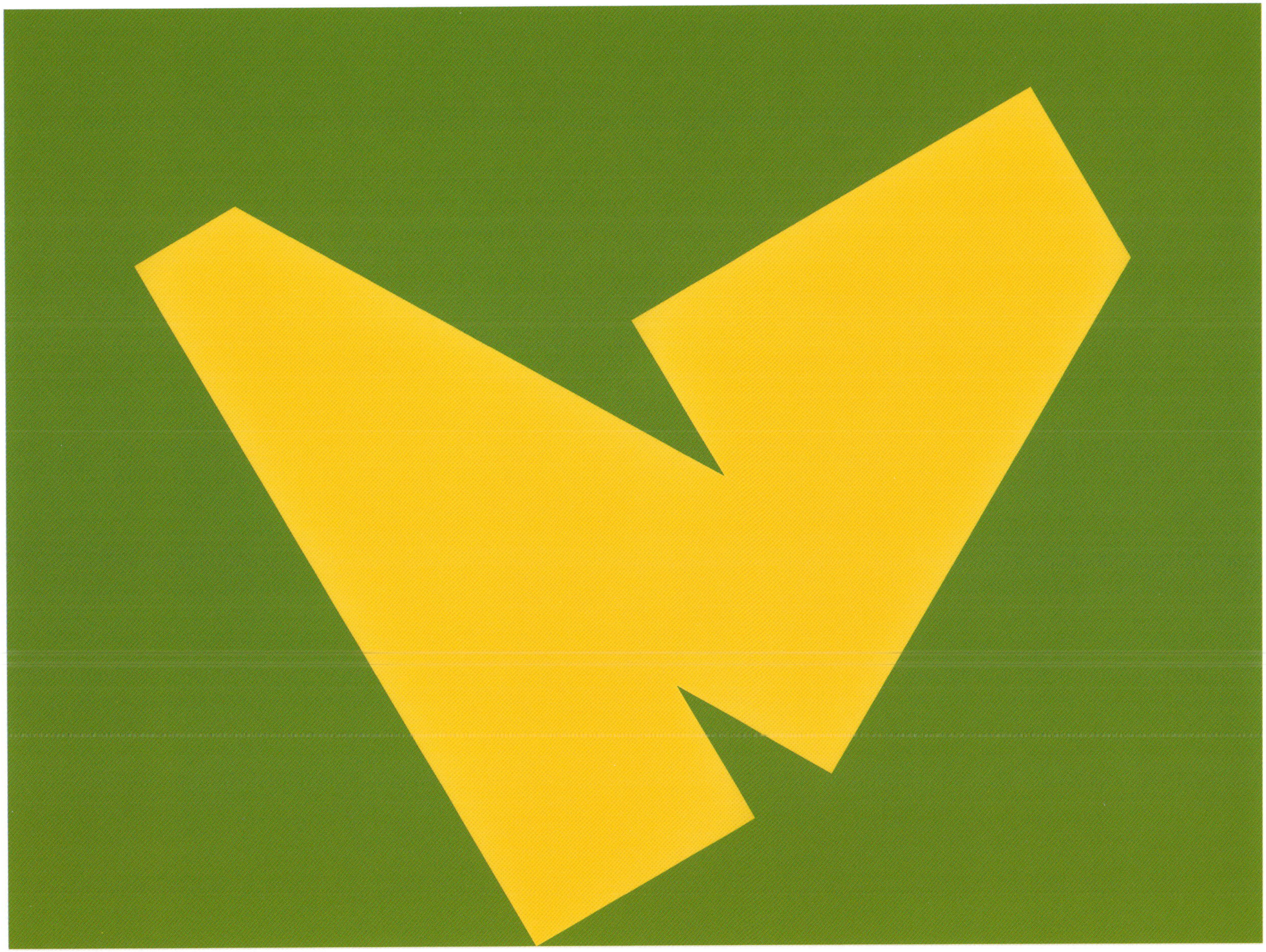

Lubin, 2002, 72" x 95 5/8", Acrylic on Canvas

Adelaide, 1998, 22" x 19 1/4", Oil on Canvas

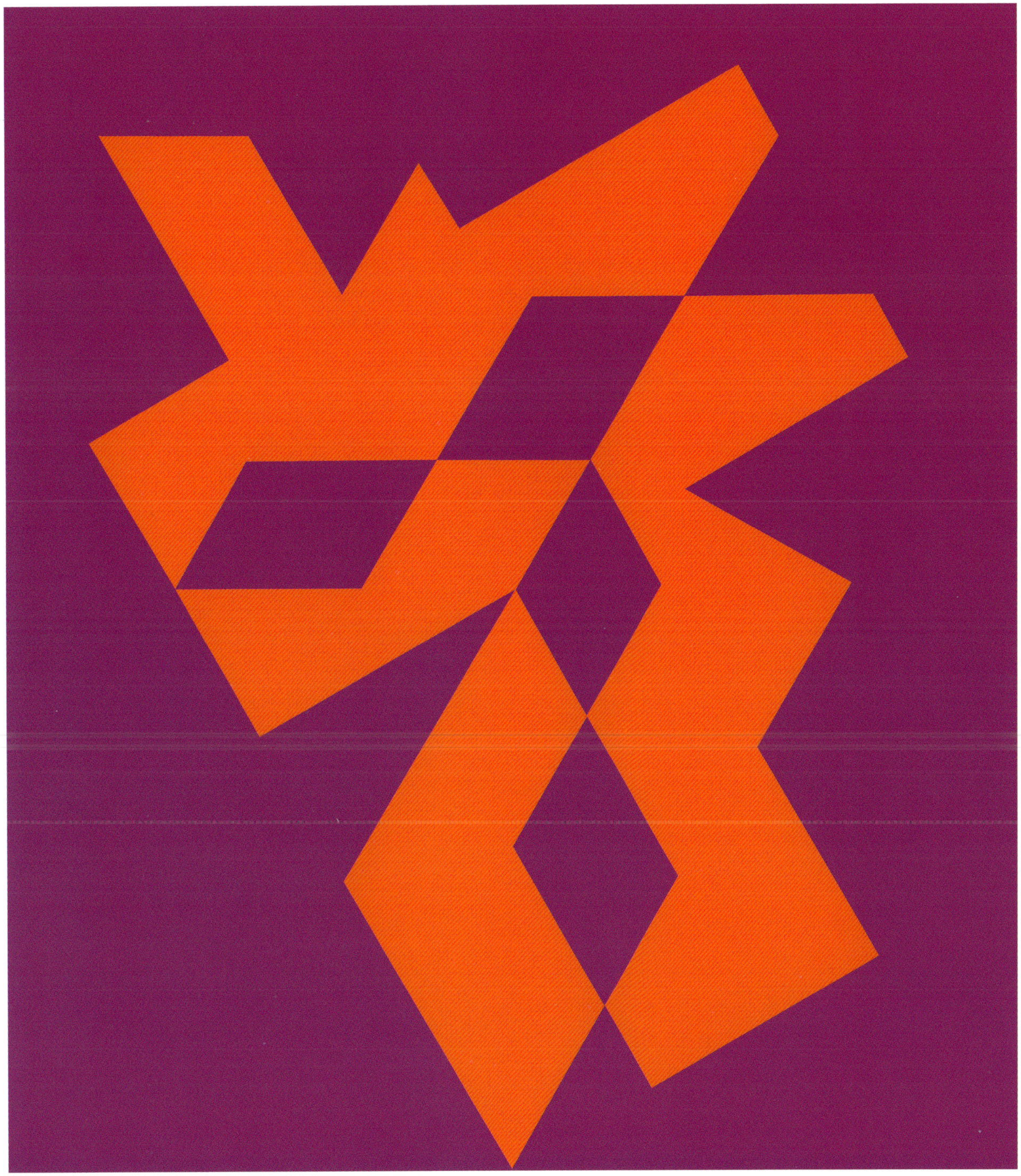

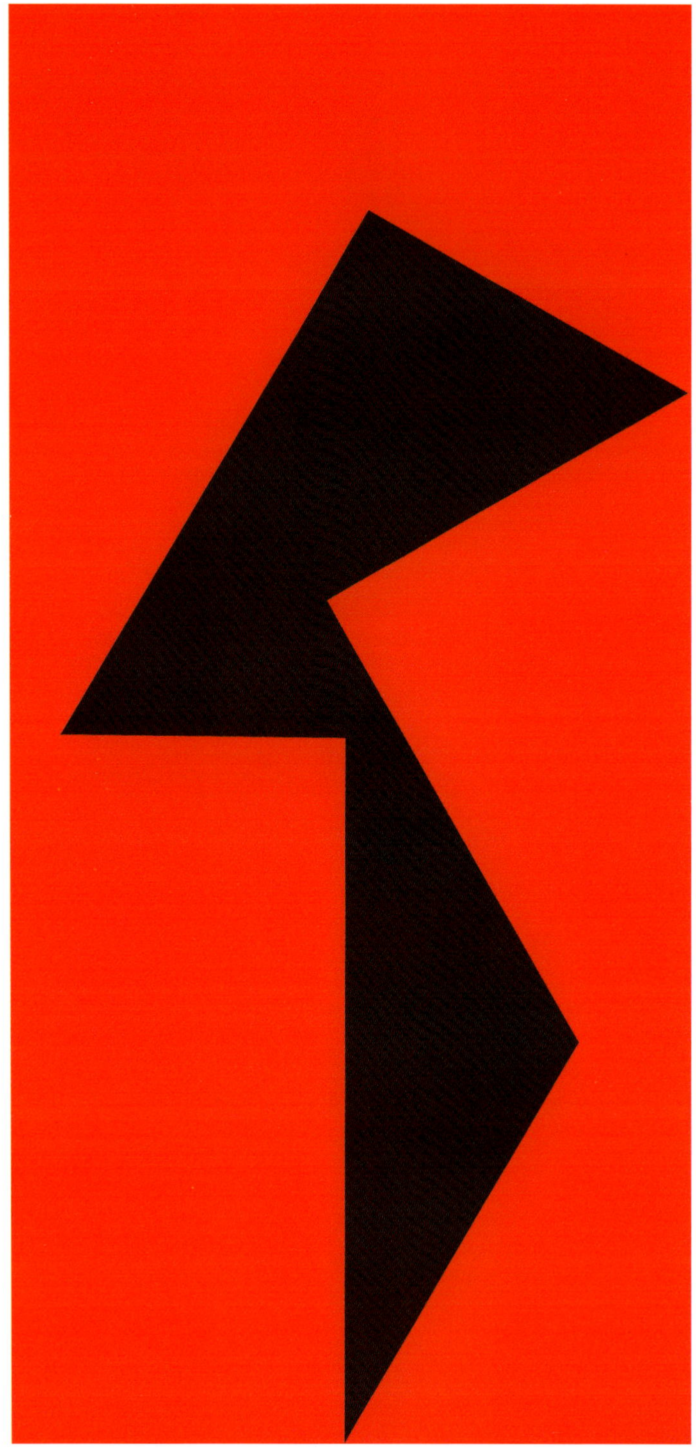

BJB, 1998, 25" x 11 3/4", Acrylic on Canvas

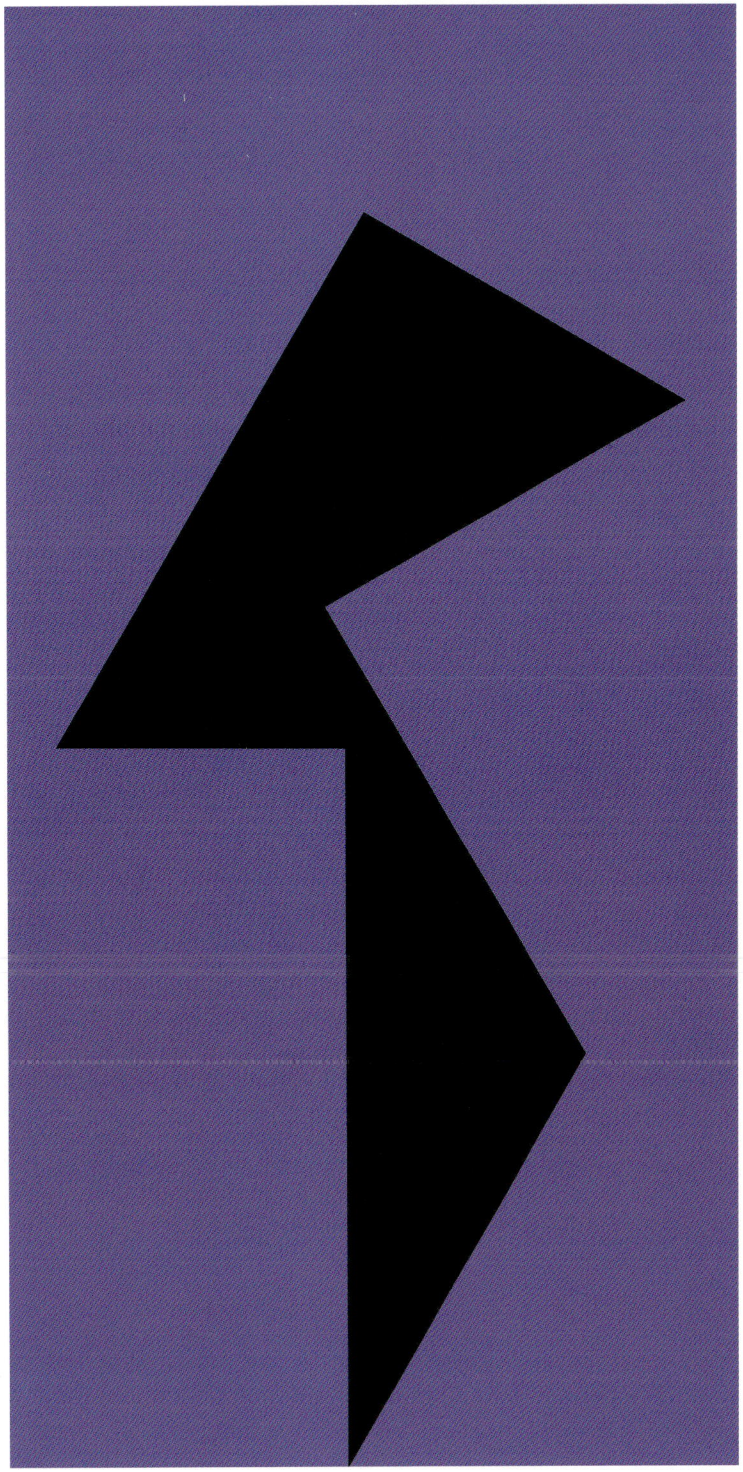

Damian, 2004, 67 1/4" x 33 5/8", Acrylic on Canvas

ISCHYRION, 2004, 74 7/8" x 74 1/4", Acrylic on Canvas

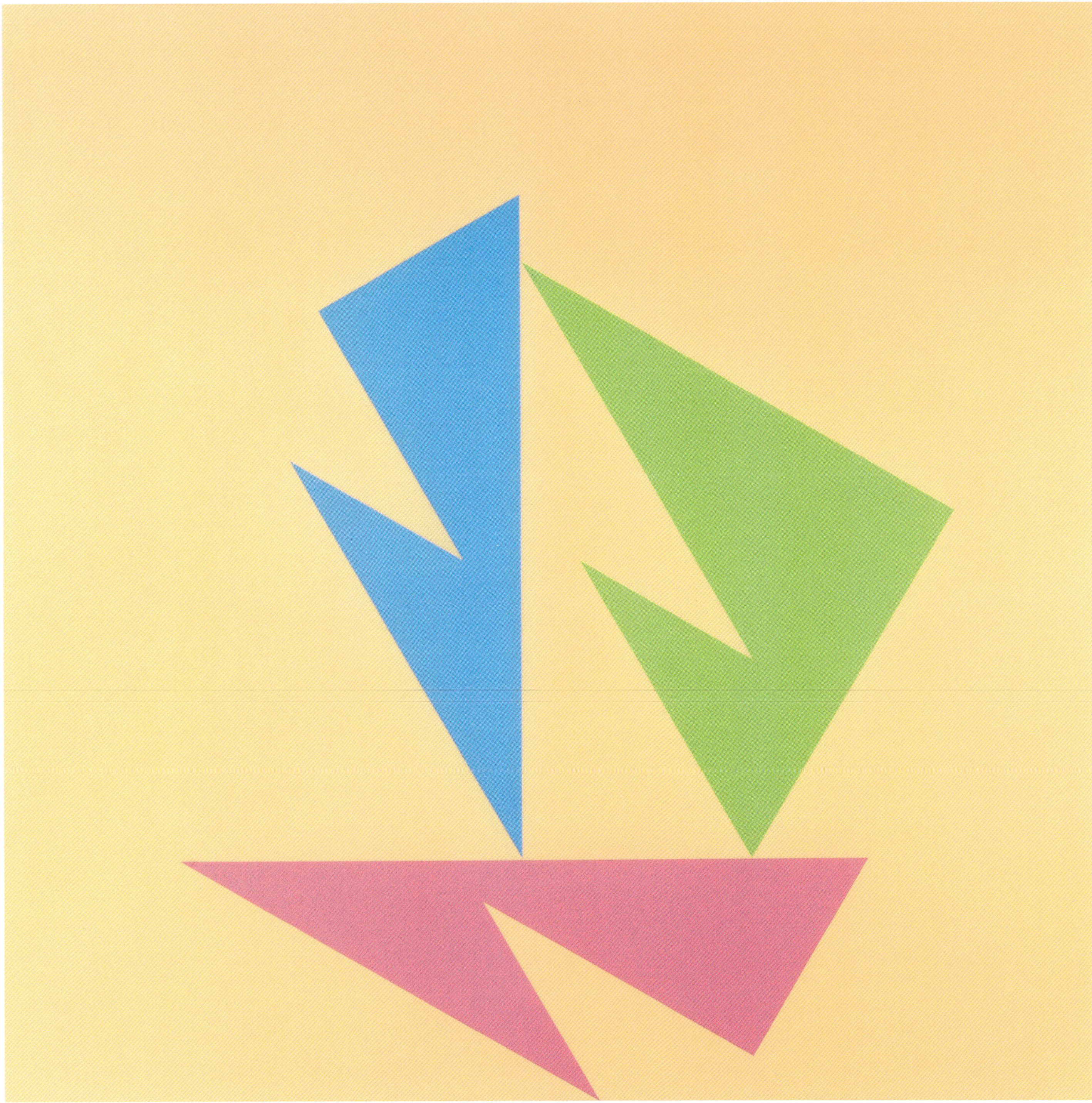

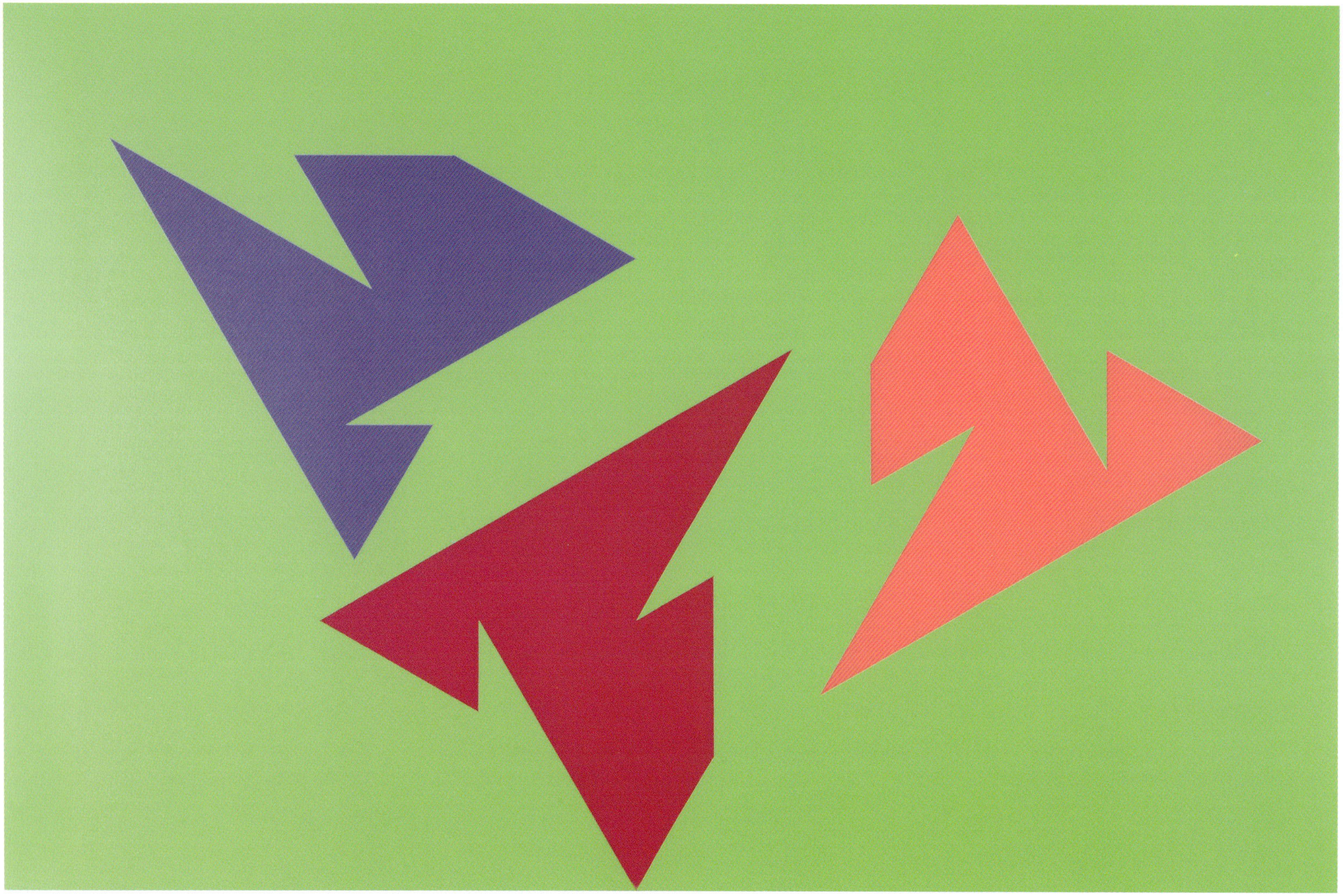

Magi, 2005, 59 1/4" x 88 5/8", Acrylic on Canvas

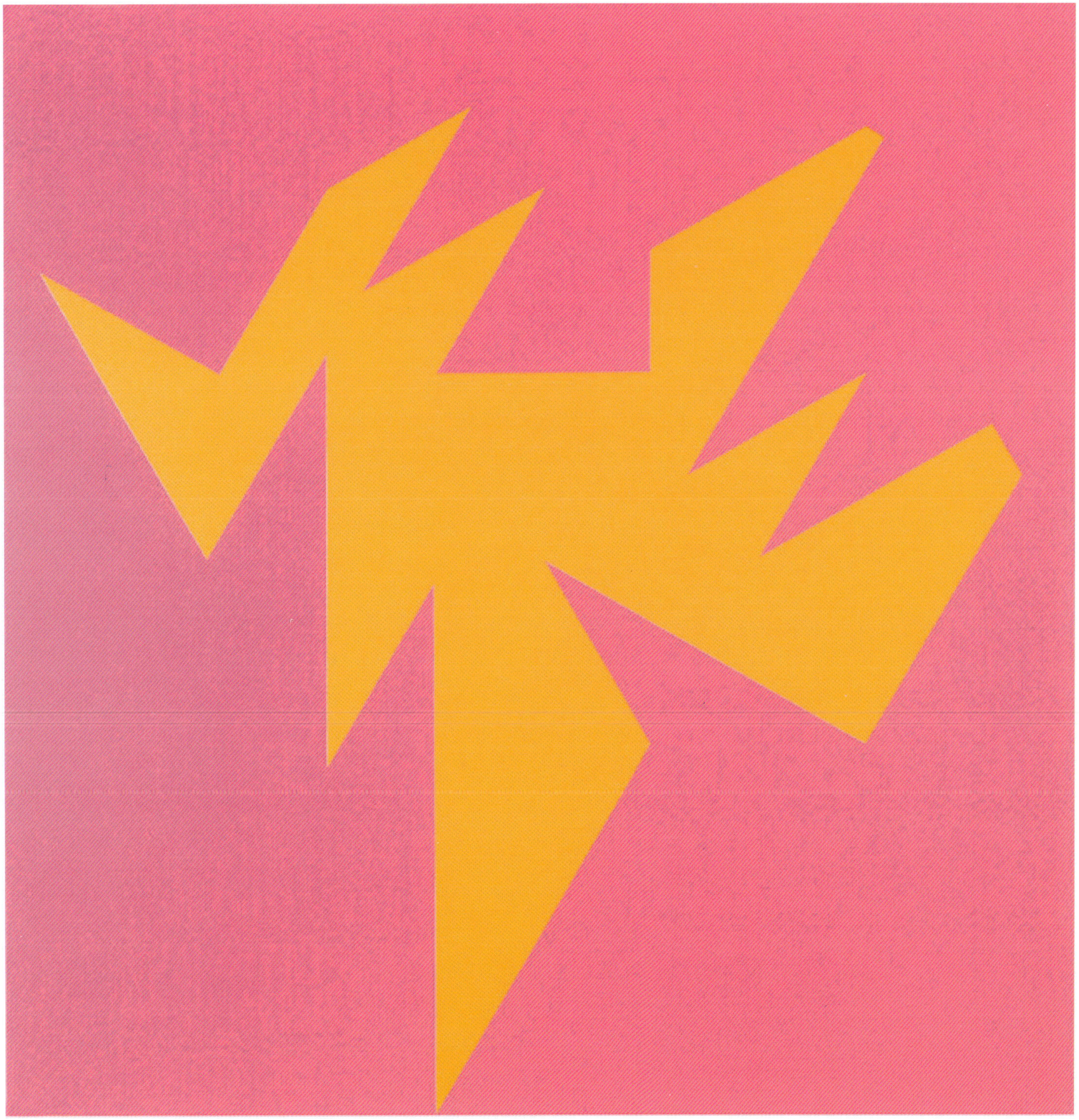

Karol, 2005, 67 3/4" x 65 1/8", Acrylic on Canvas

EUDES, 2006, 51 3/4" x 95 3/4", ACRYLIC ON CANVAS

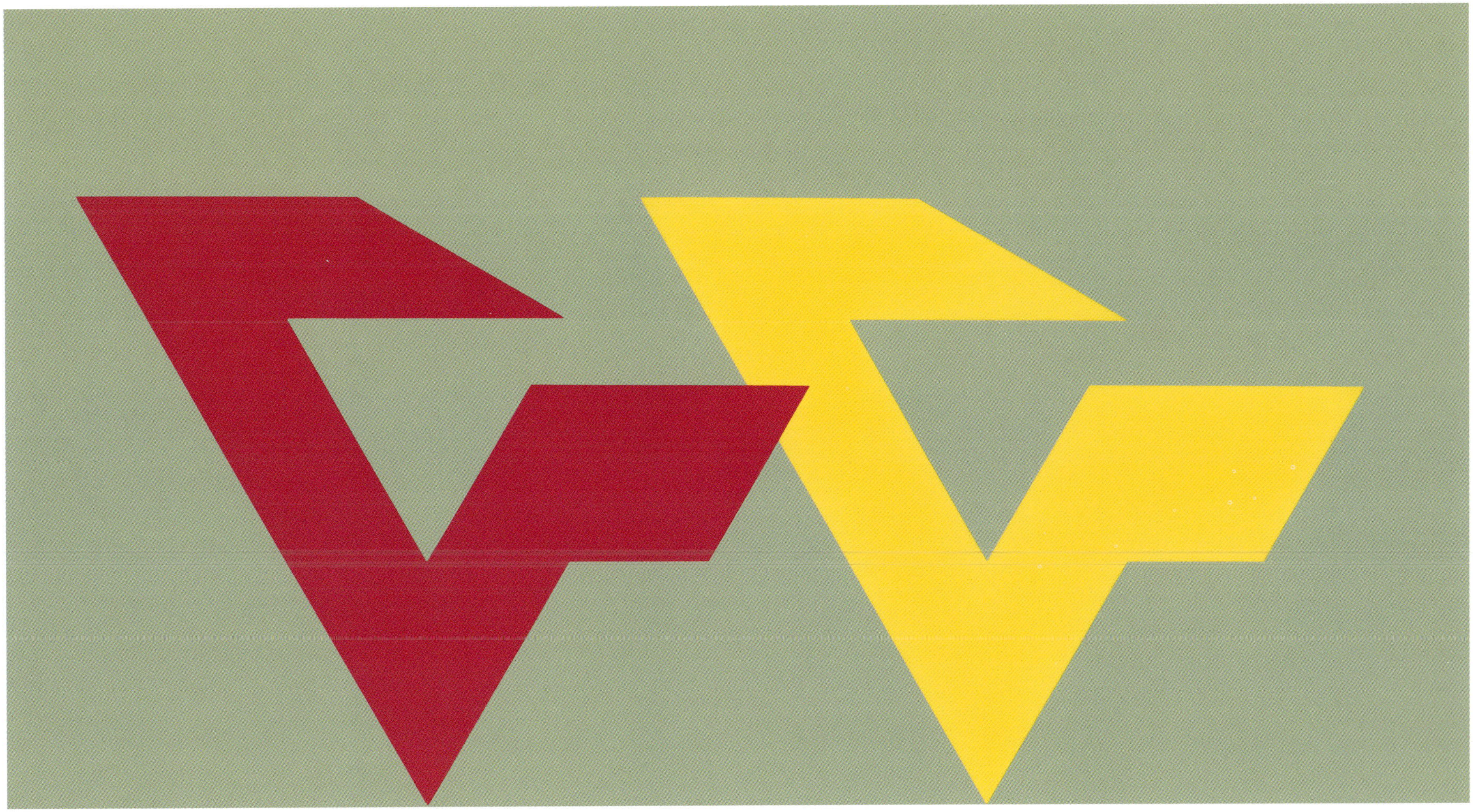

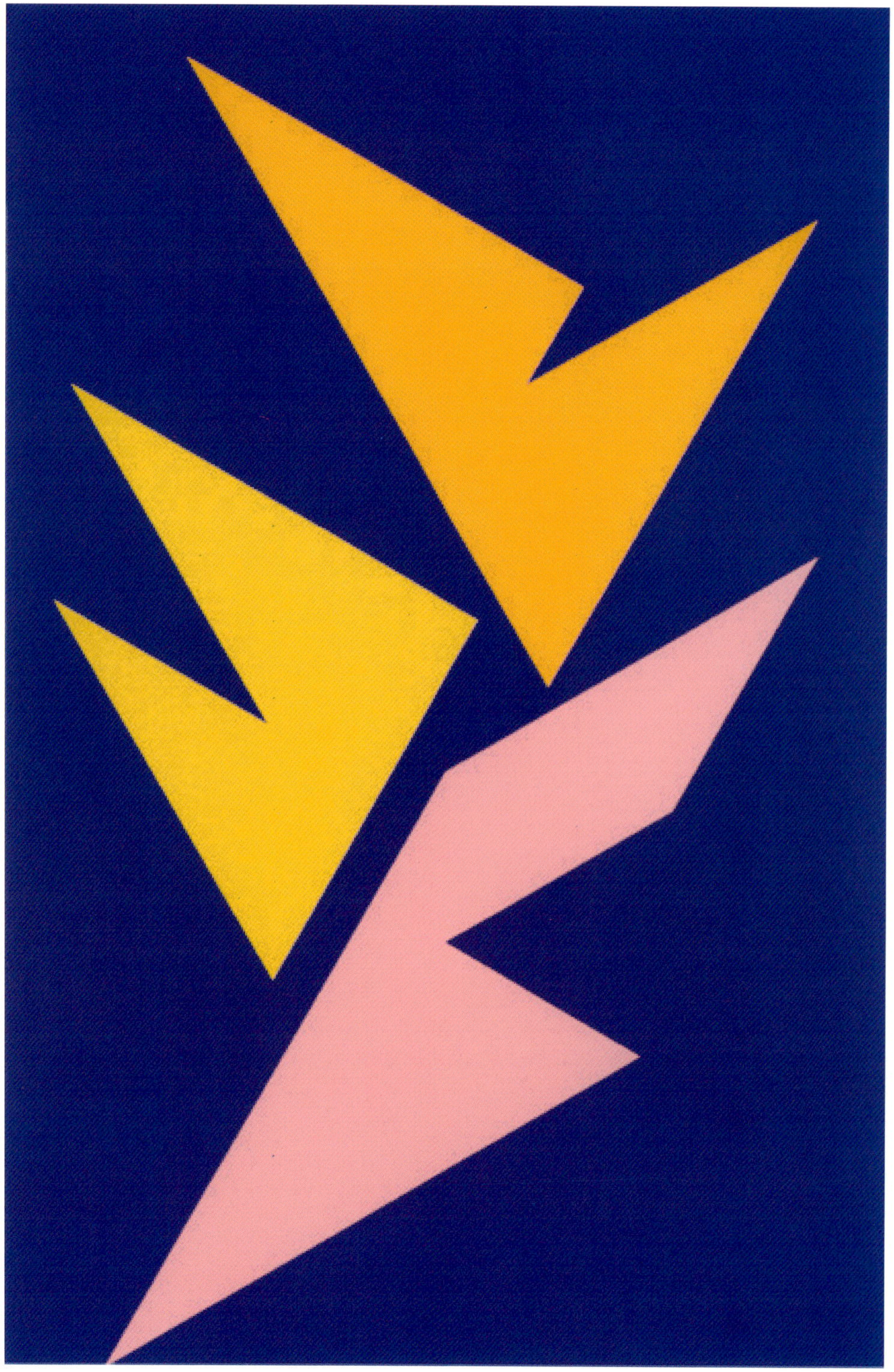

Spiridion, 2004, 89 1/2" x 58 1/2", Acrylic on Canvas

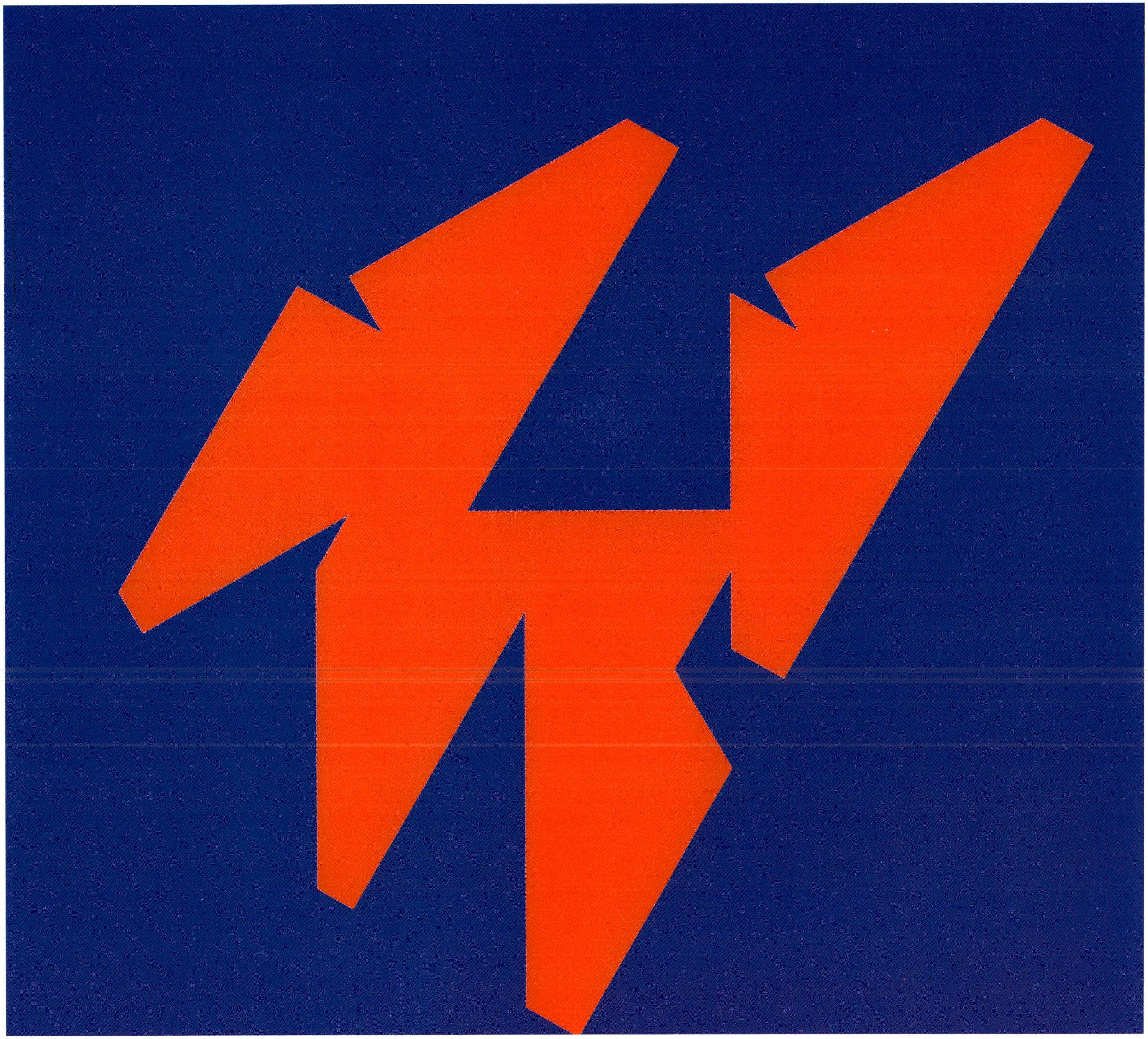

Neri, 2006, 65 3/4" x 71 5/8", Acrylic on Canvas

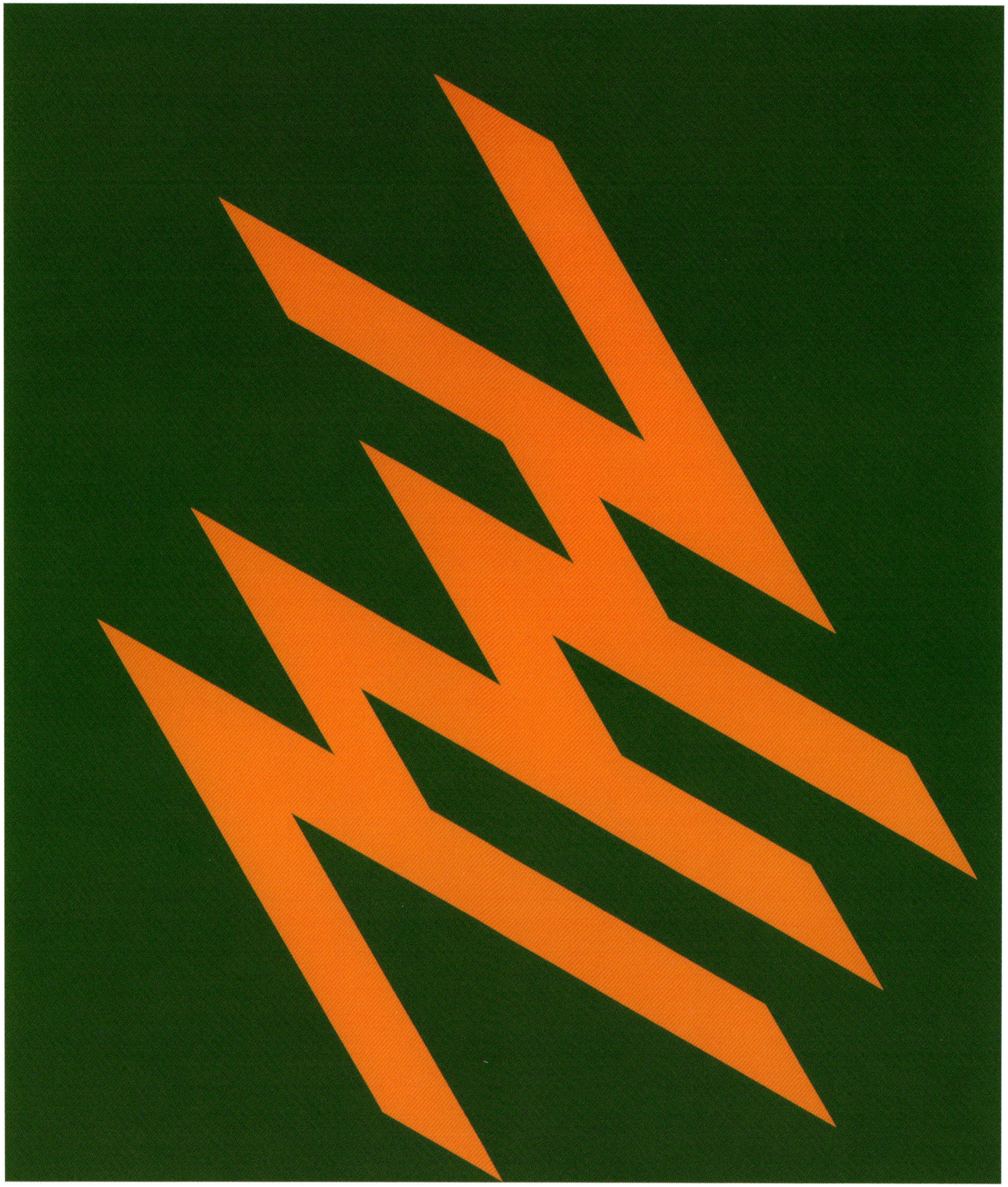

Pantaleon, 2007, 64 7/8" x 54 13/16", Acrylic on Canvas

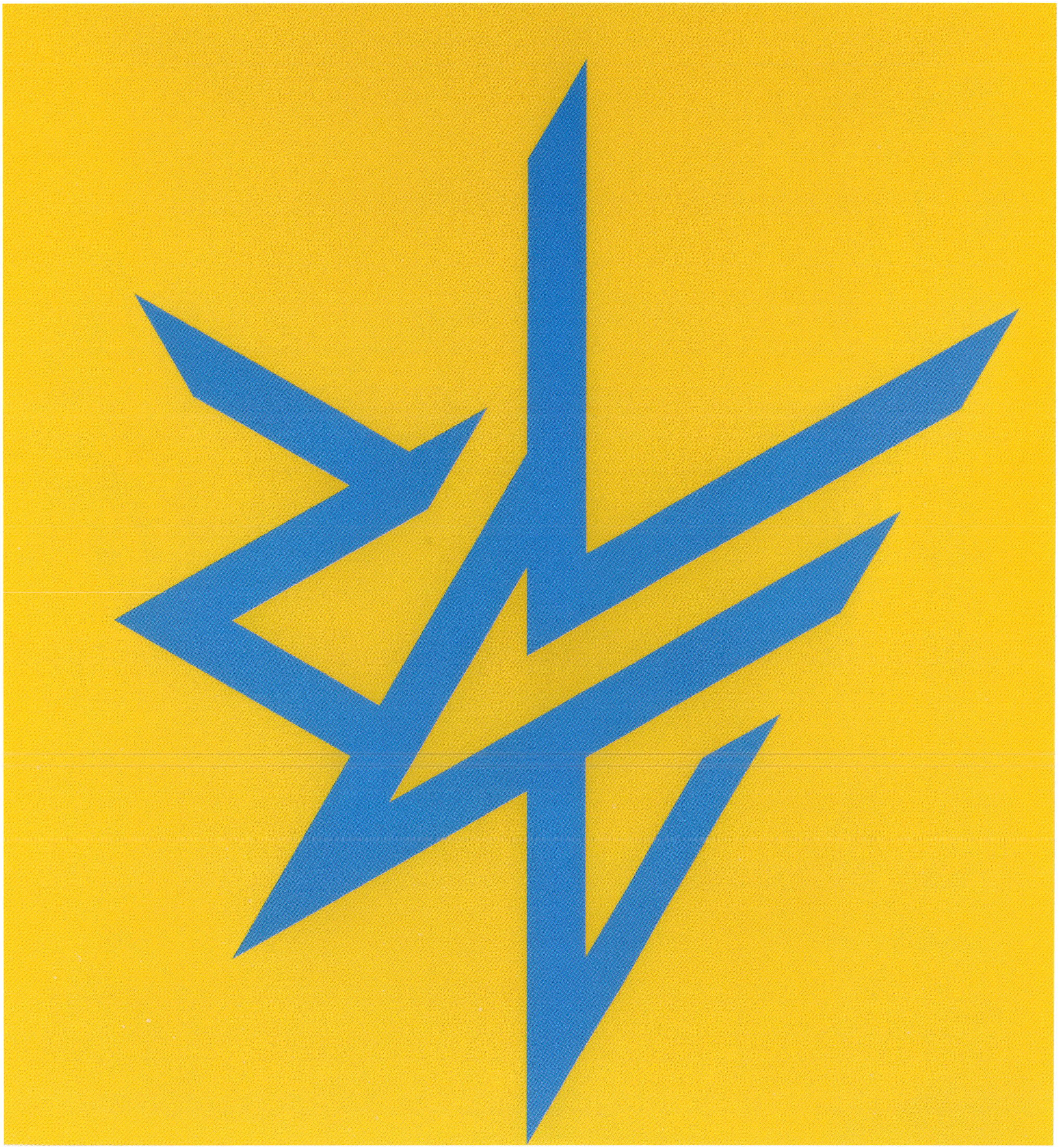

Romula, 2007, 76 5/8" x 70 3/8", Acrylic on Canvas

Olaf, 2007, 73" x 65", Acrylic on Canvas

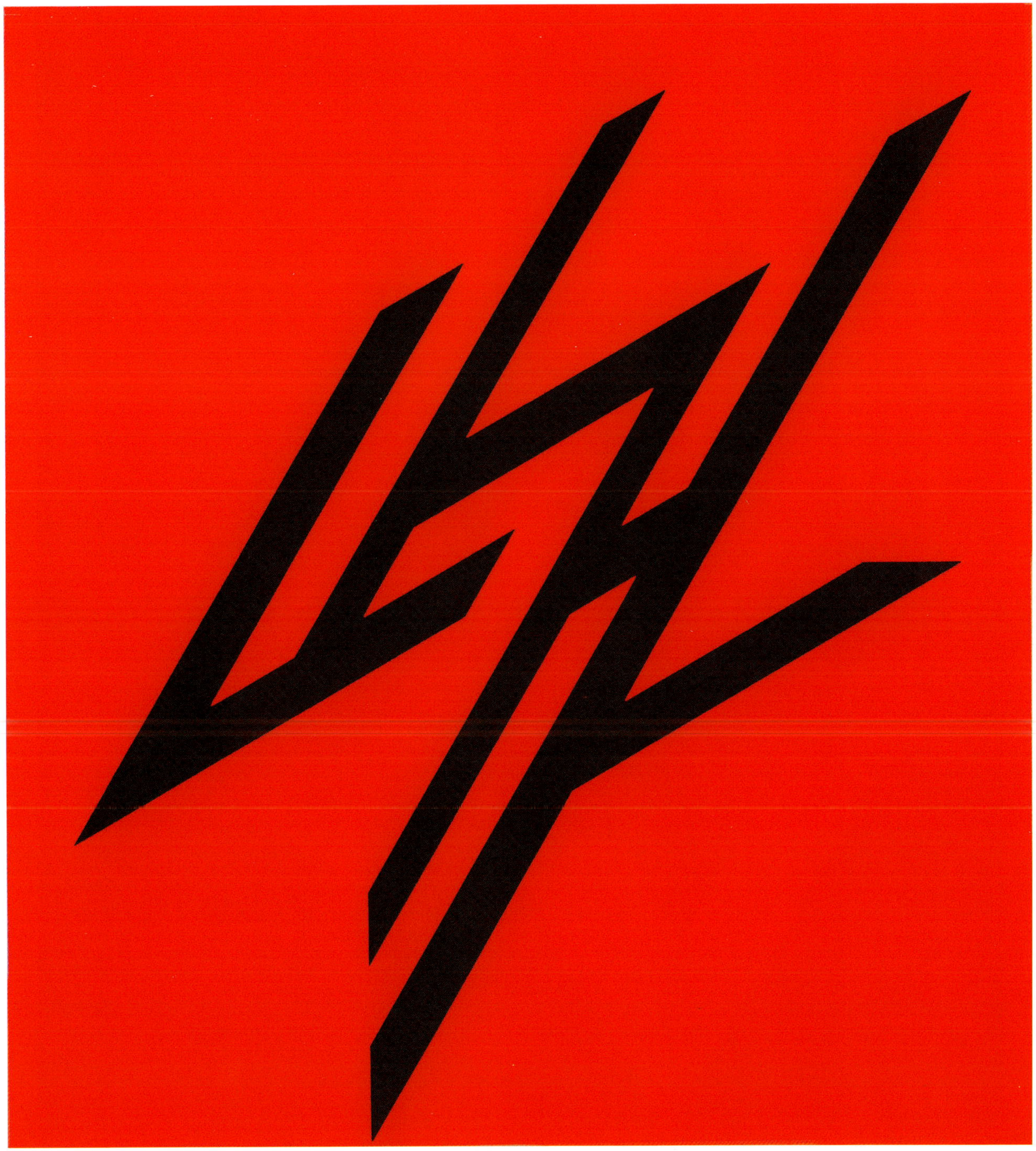

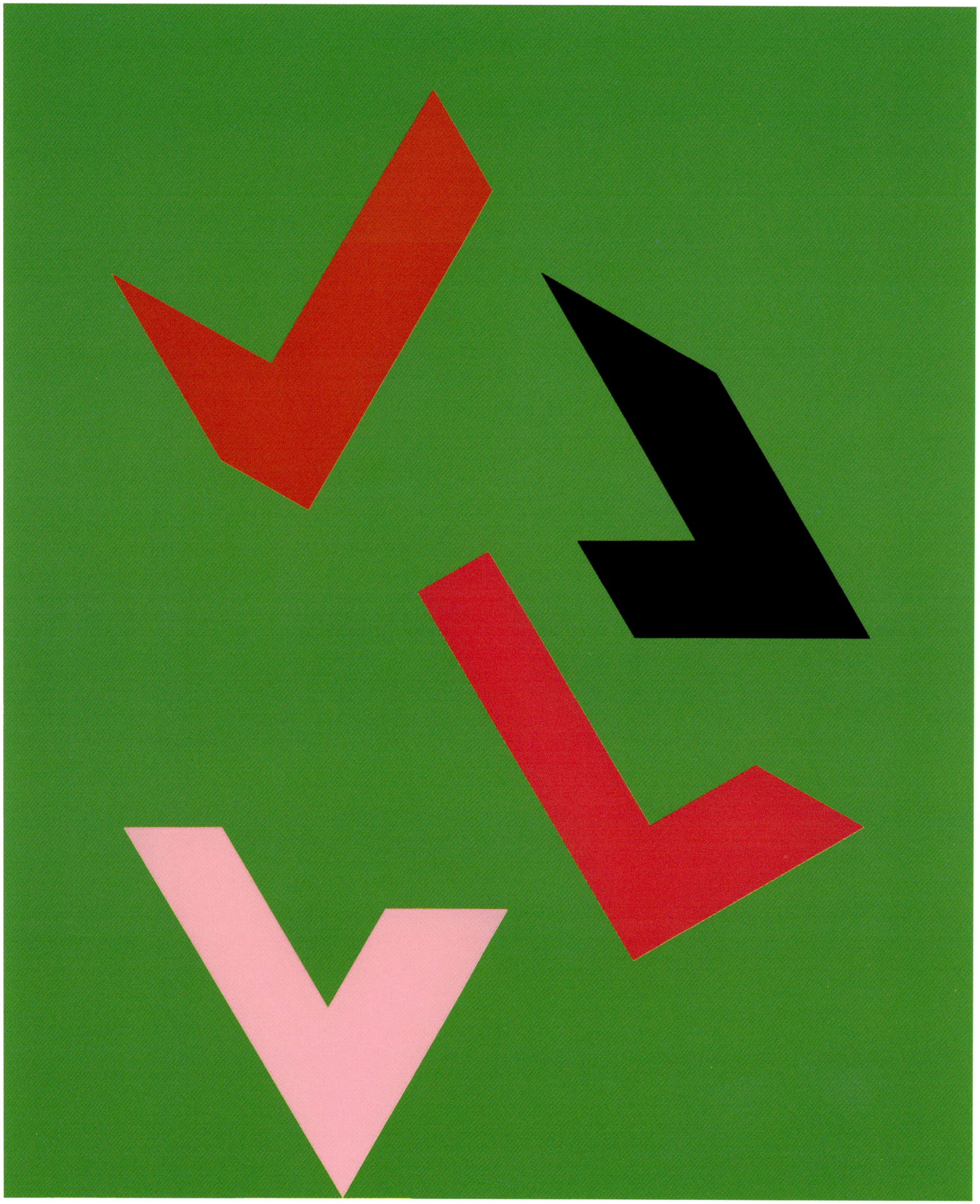

LUKE, 2008, 51" X 41 1/4", ACRYLIC ON CANVAS

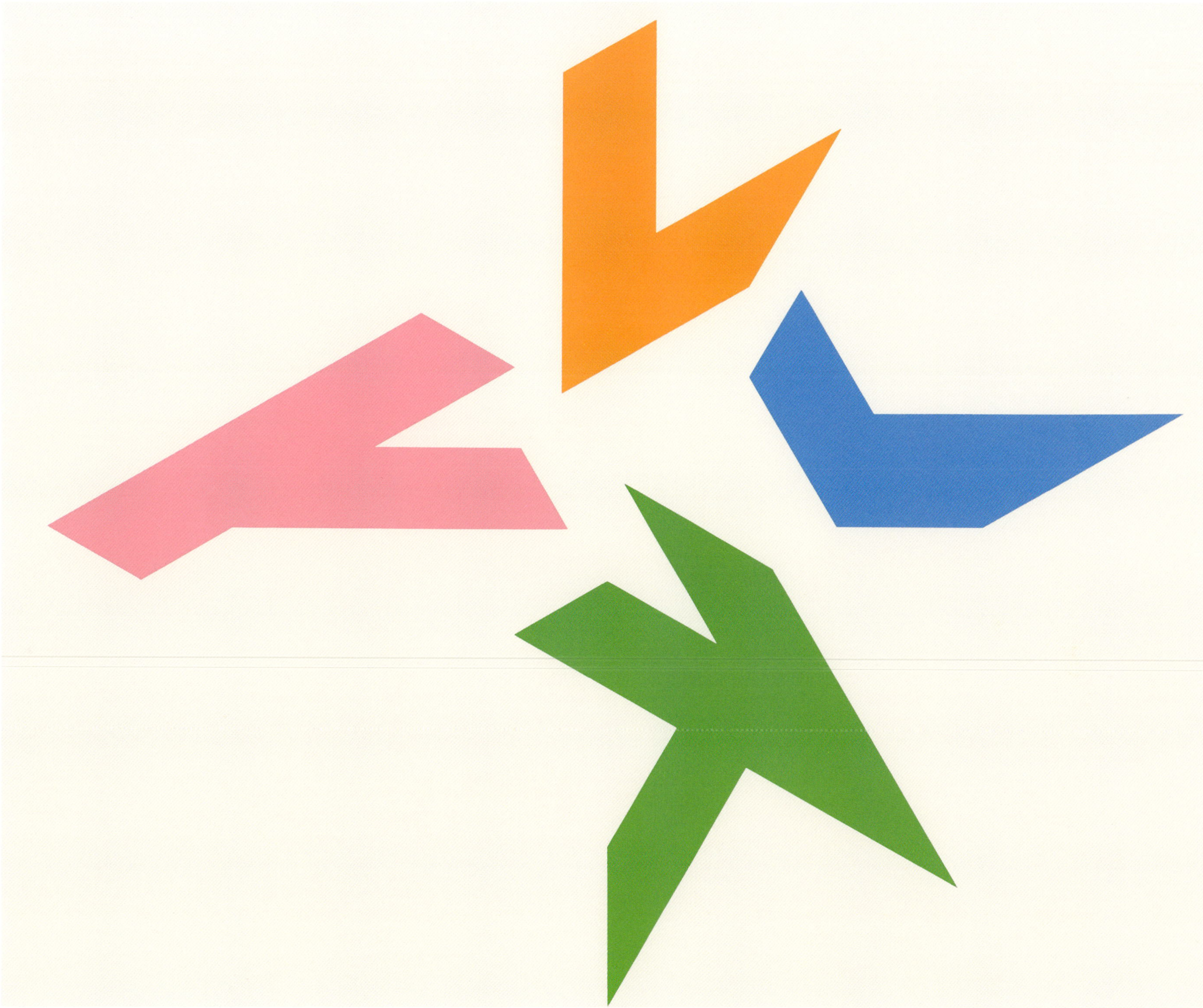

Jerome, 2008, 42" x 50 3/8", Acrylic on Canvas

CELSUS, 2007, 70 7/8" x 86", ACRYLIC ON CANVAS

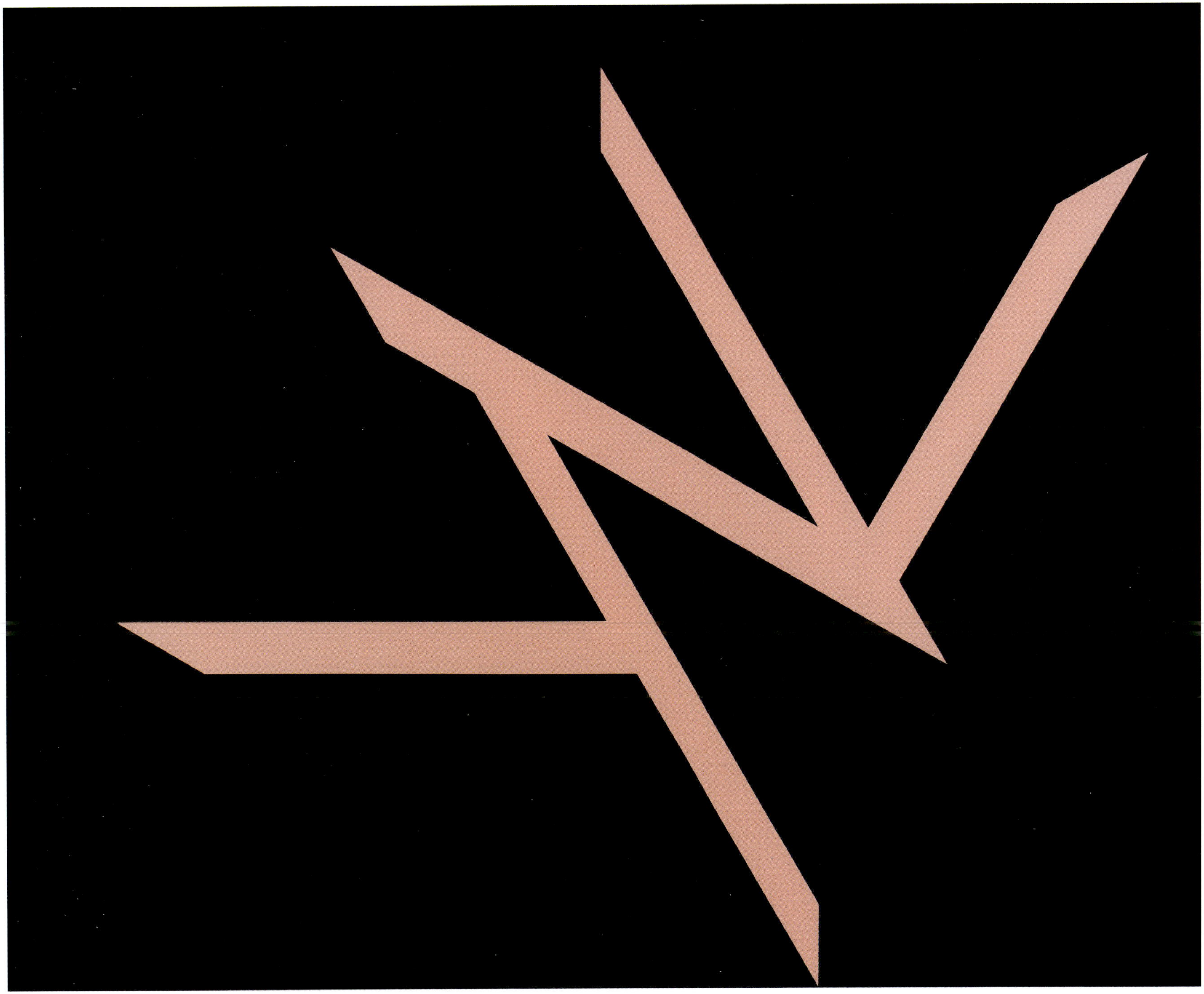

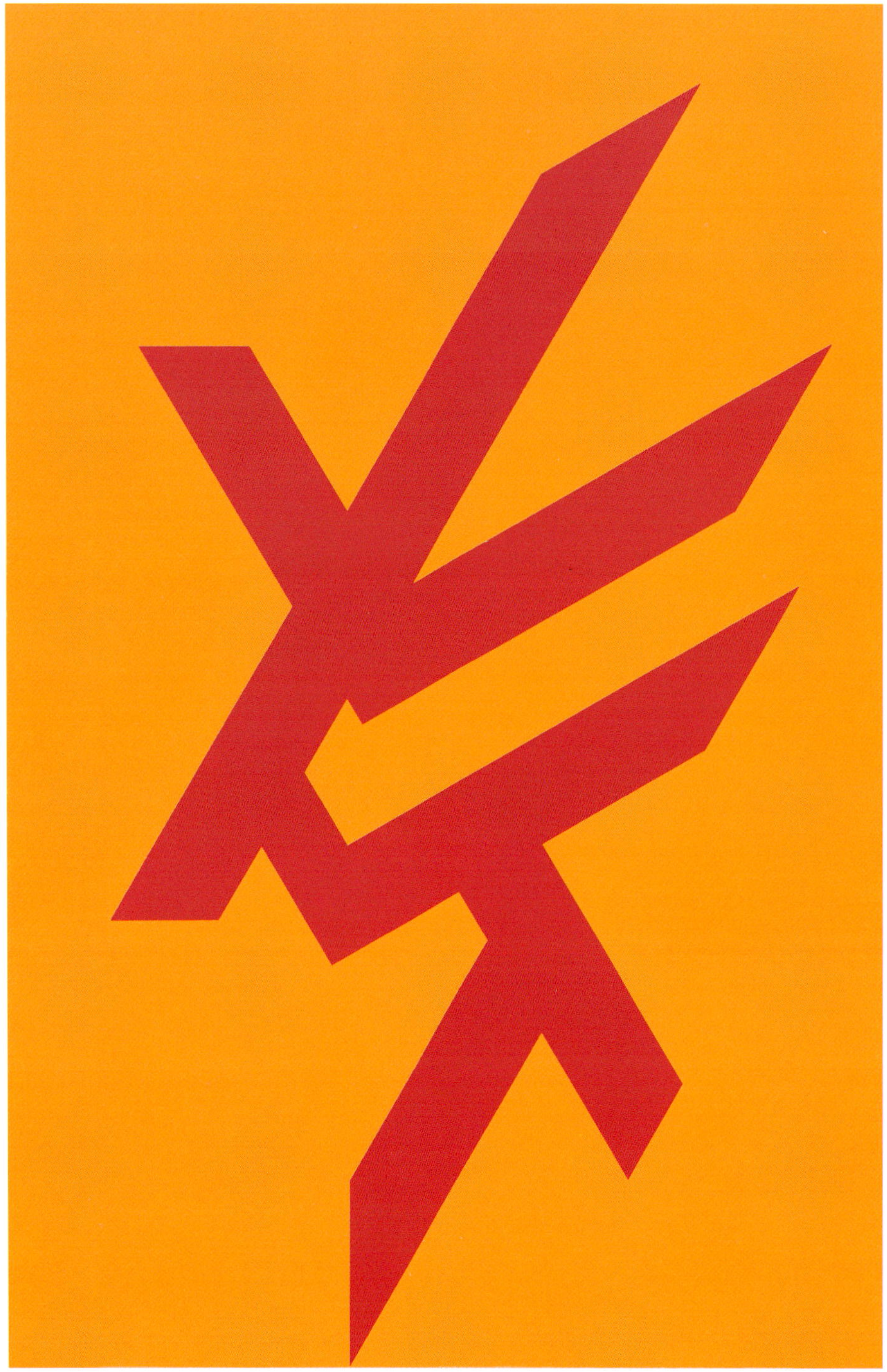

EDWARD (3), 2008, 55" X 35 1/4", ACRYLIC ON CANVAS

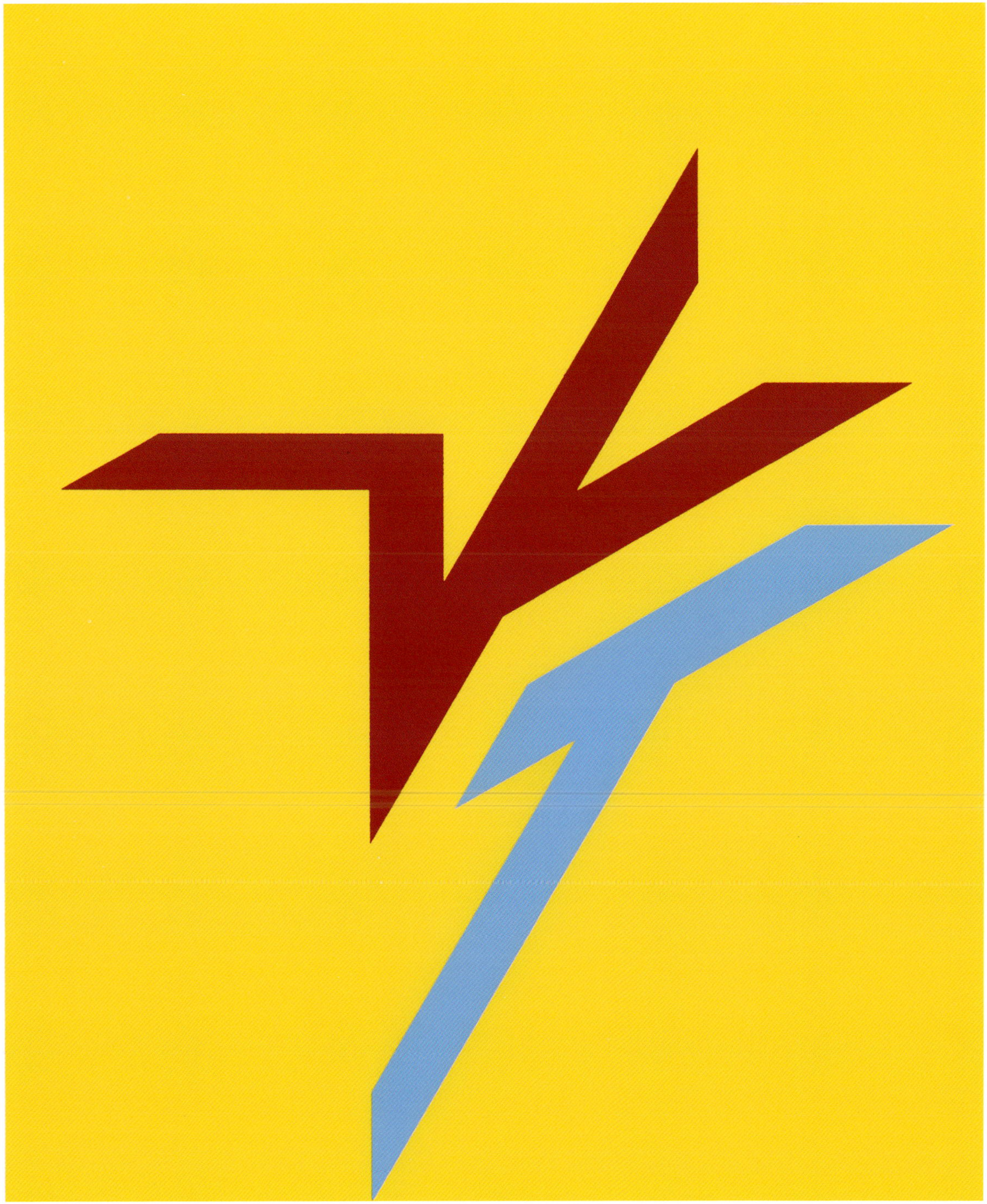

Aleksandr (2), 2008, 42 7/8" x 35", Acrylic on Canvas

Cathedra, 2008, 58 1/4" x 55", Acrylic on Canvas

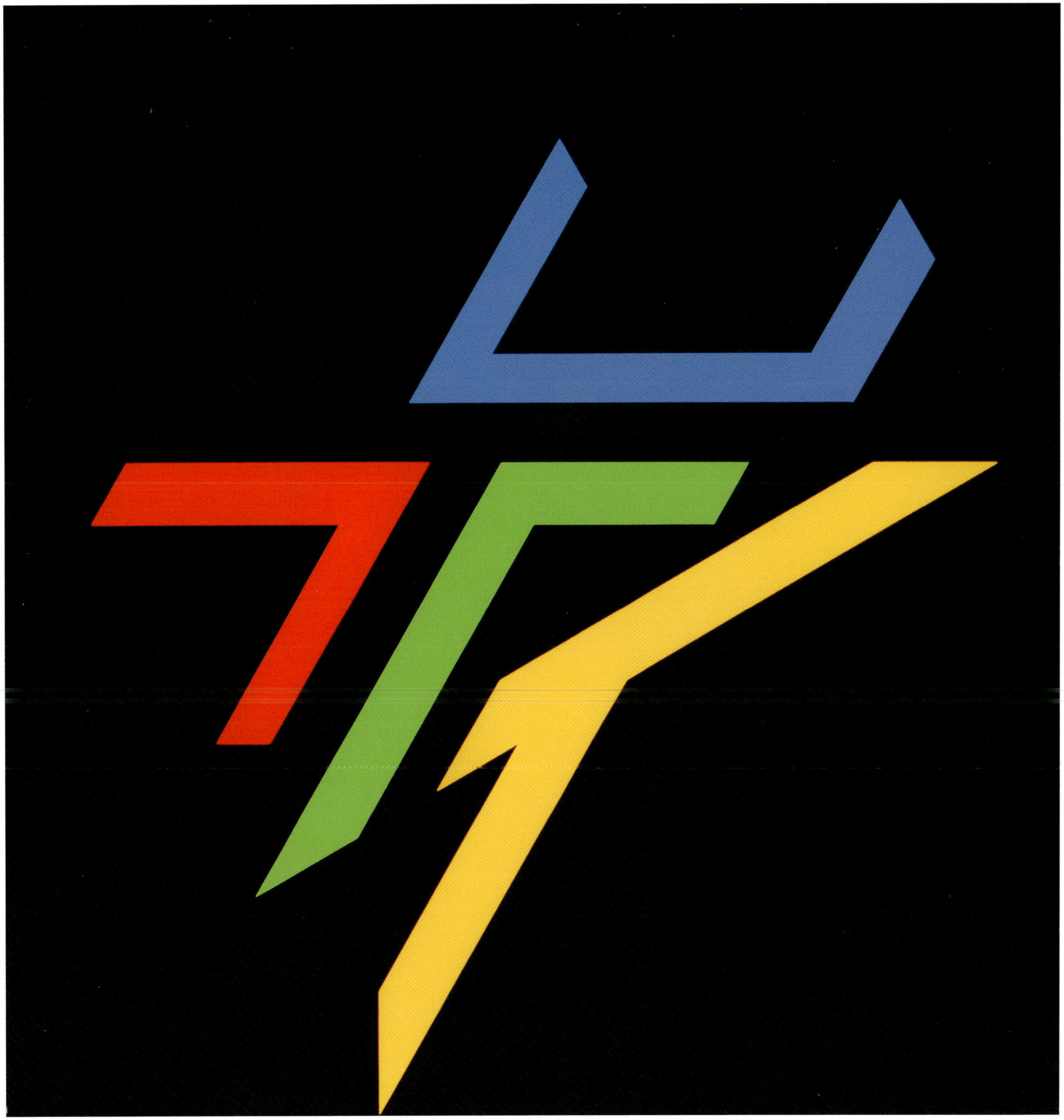

Leonides, 2009, 41 1/8" x 62 5/8", Acrylic on Canvas

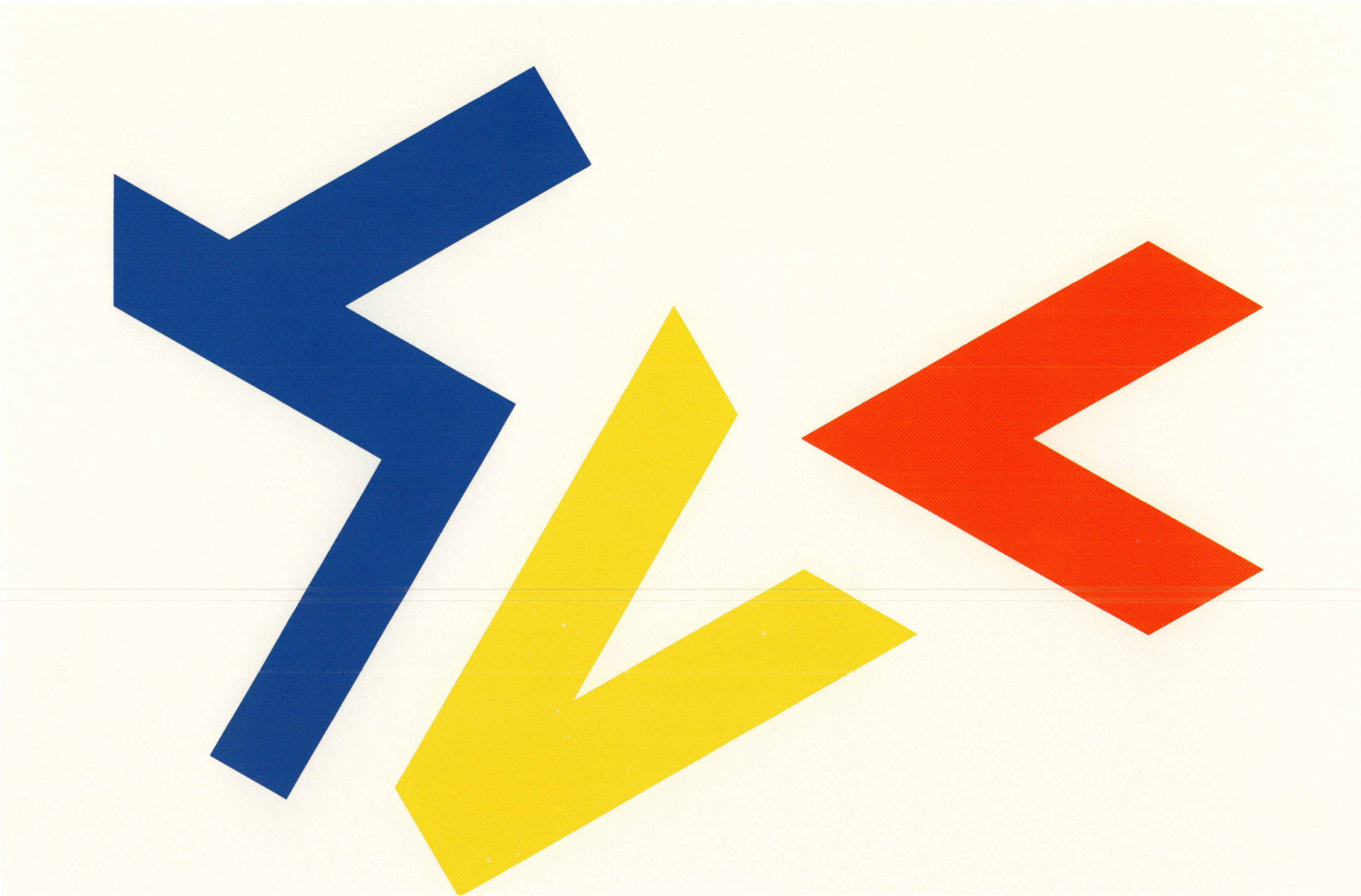

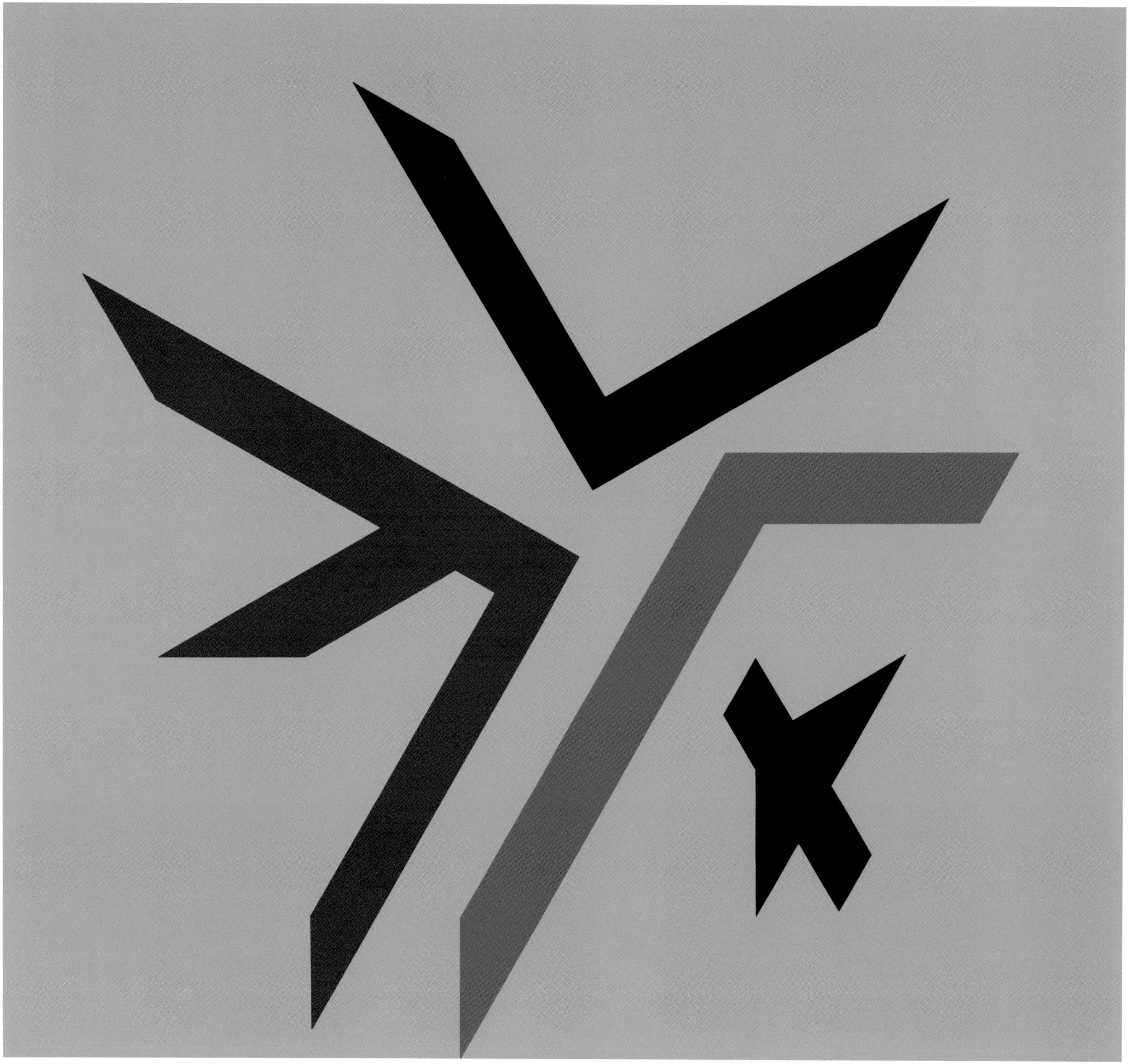

Lucian, 2010, 64 1/2" x 68 1/2", Acrylic on Canvas

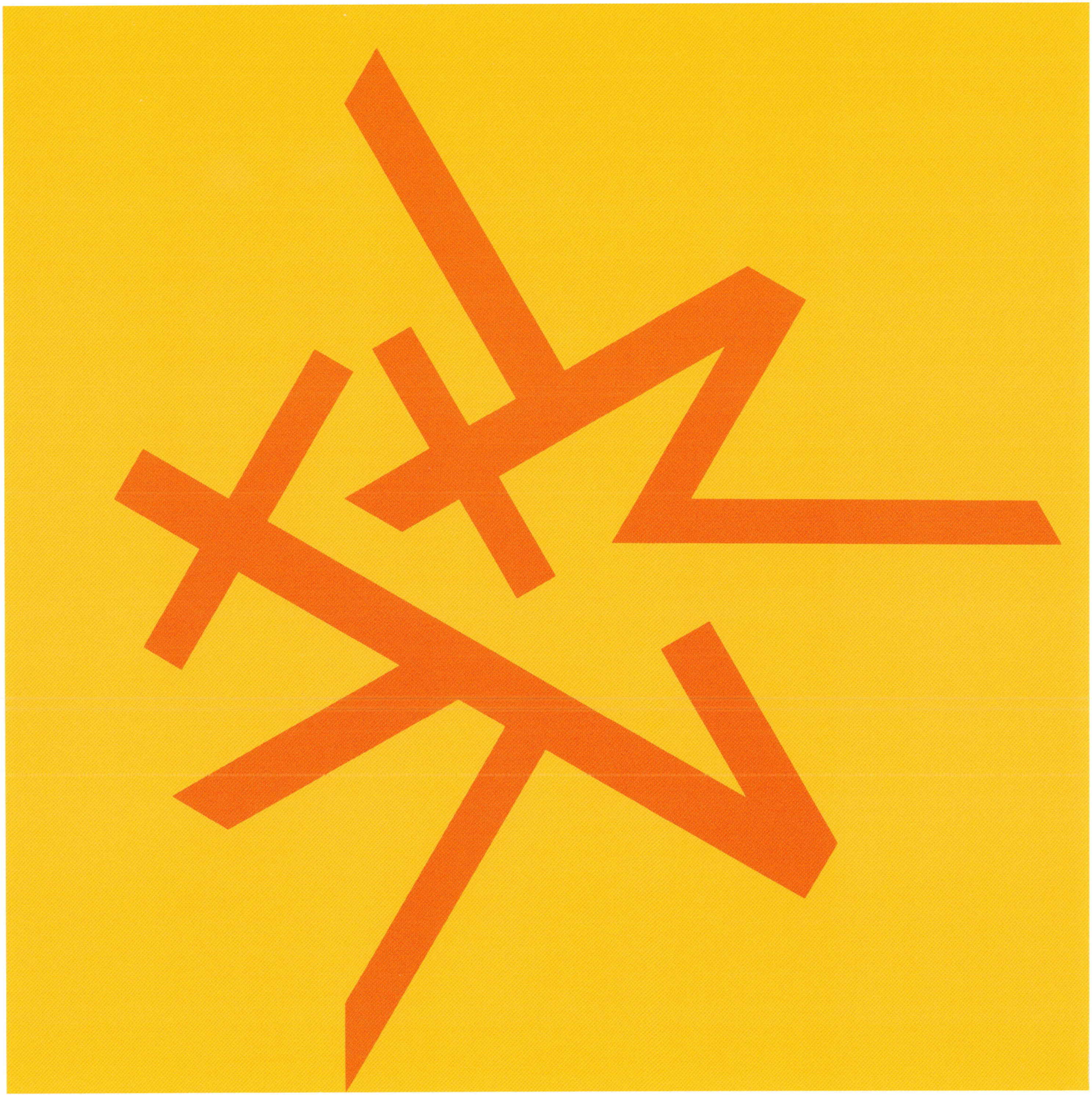

M.P.B., 2010, 74 1/2" x 74", Acrylic on Canvas

MARCELLINUS, 2010, 50 1/4" x 67 3/4", Acrylic on Canvas

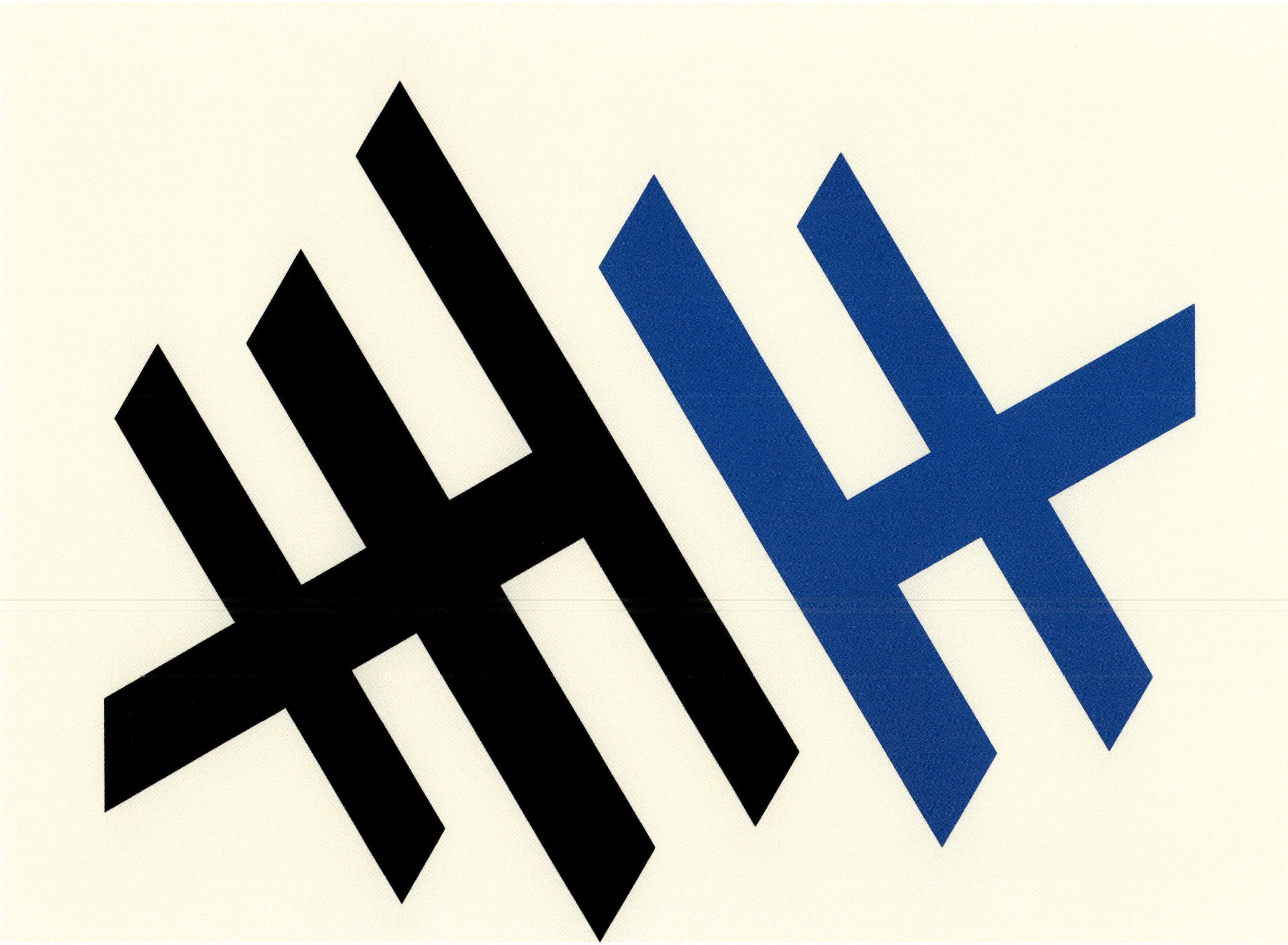

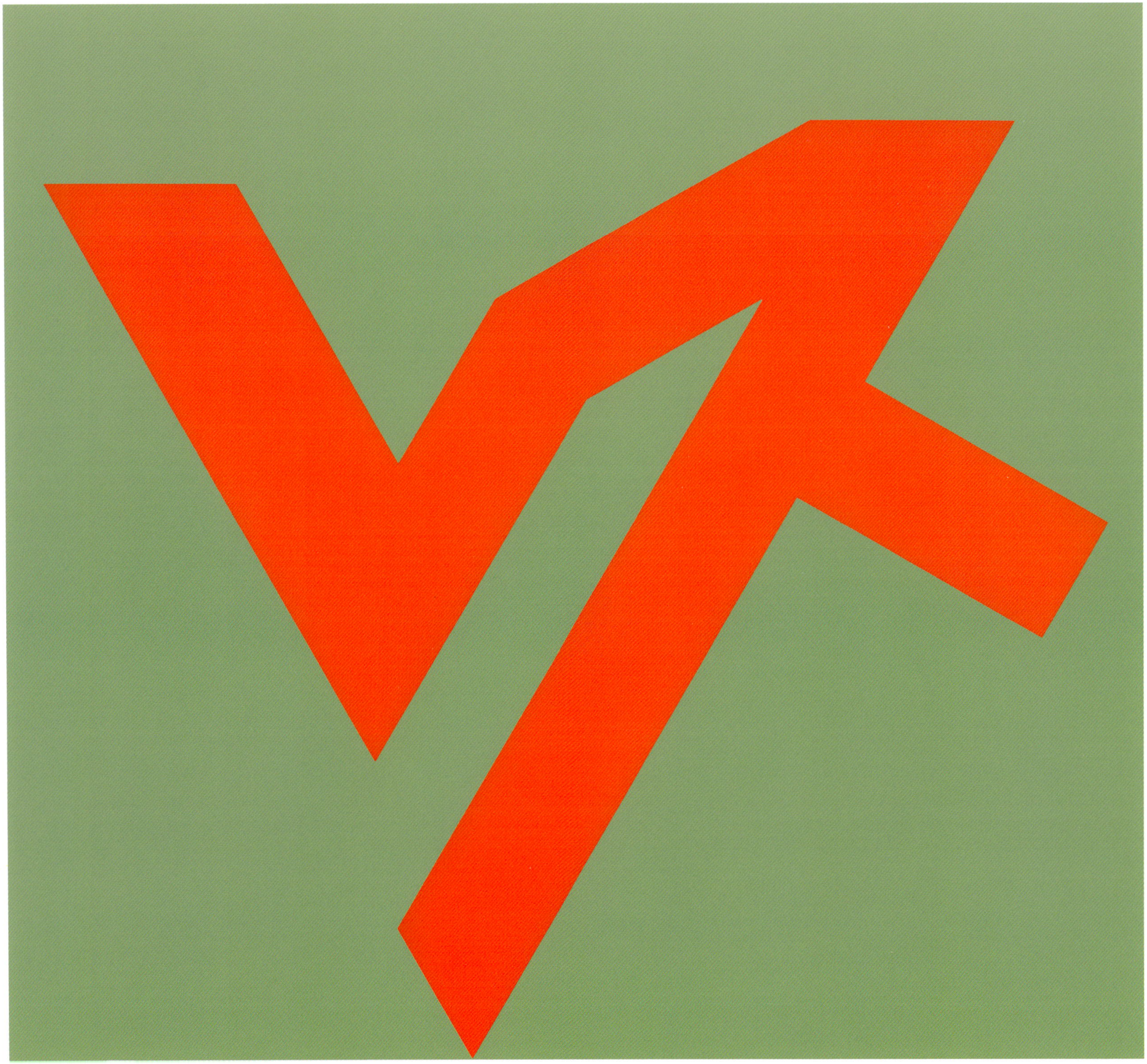

AQUILA, 2011, 62" x 66 3/8", ACRYLIC ON CANVAS

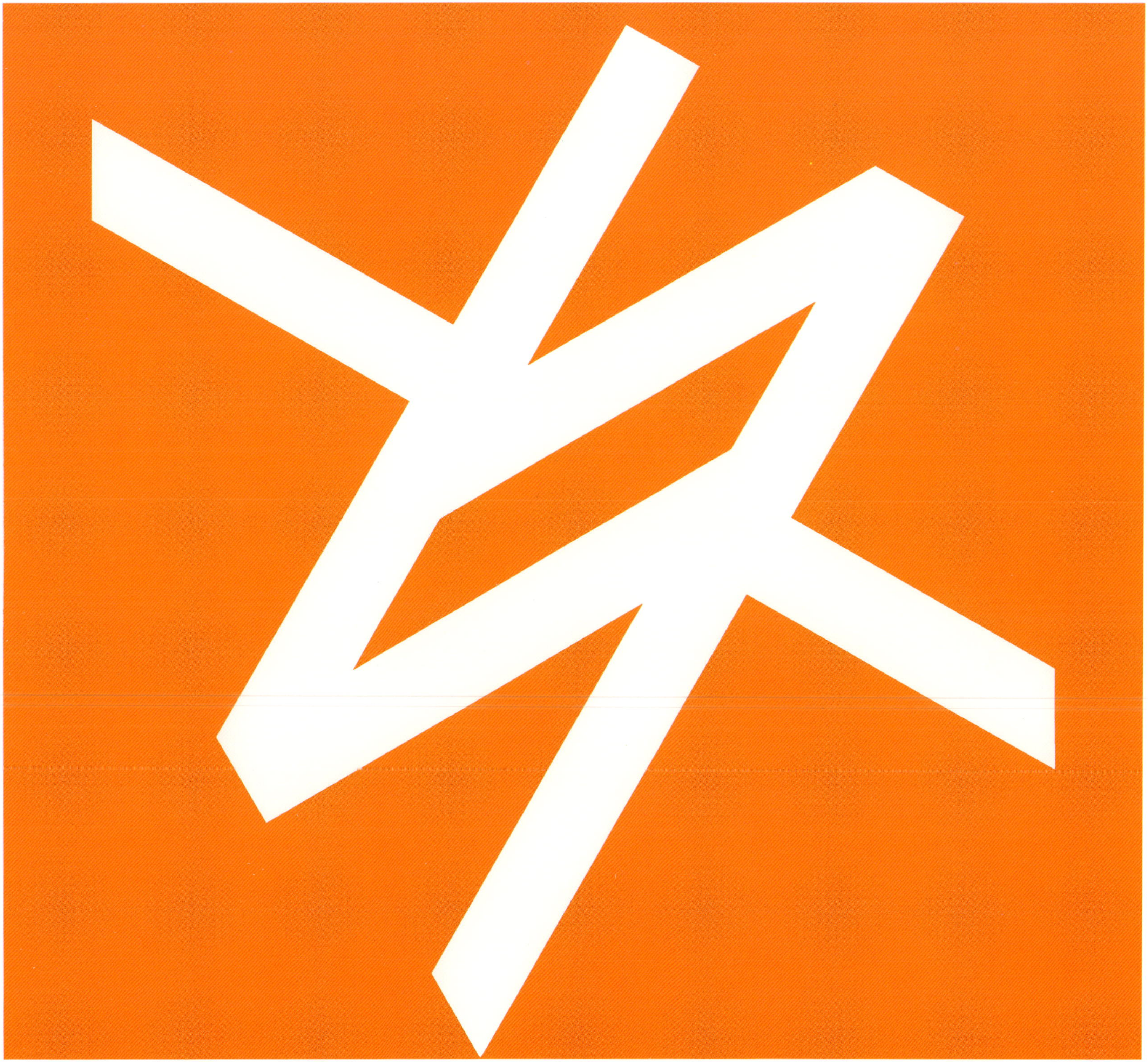

JOSEPH, 2011, 63 1/4" x 67 3/4", Acrylic on Canvas

Marcian, 2011, 50 3/8" x 65 1/2", Acrylic on Canvas

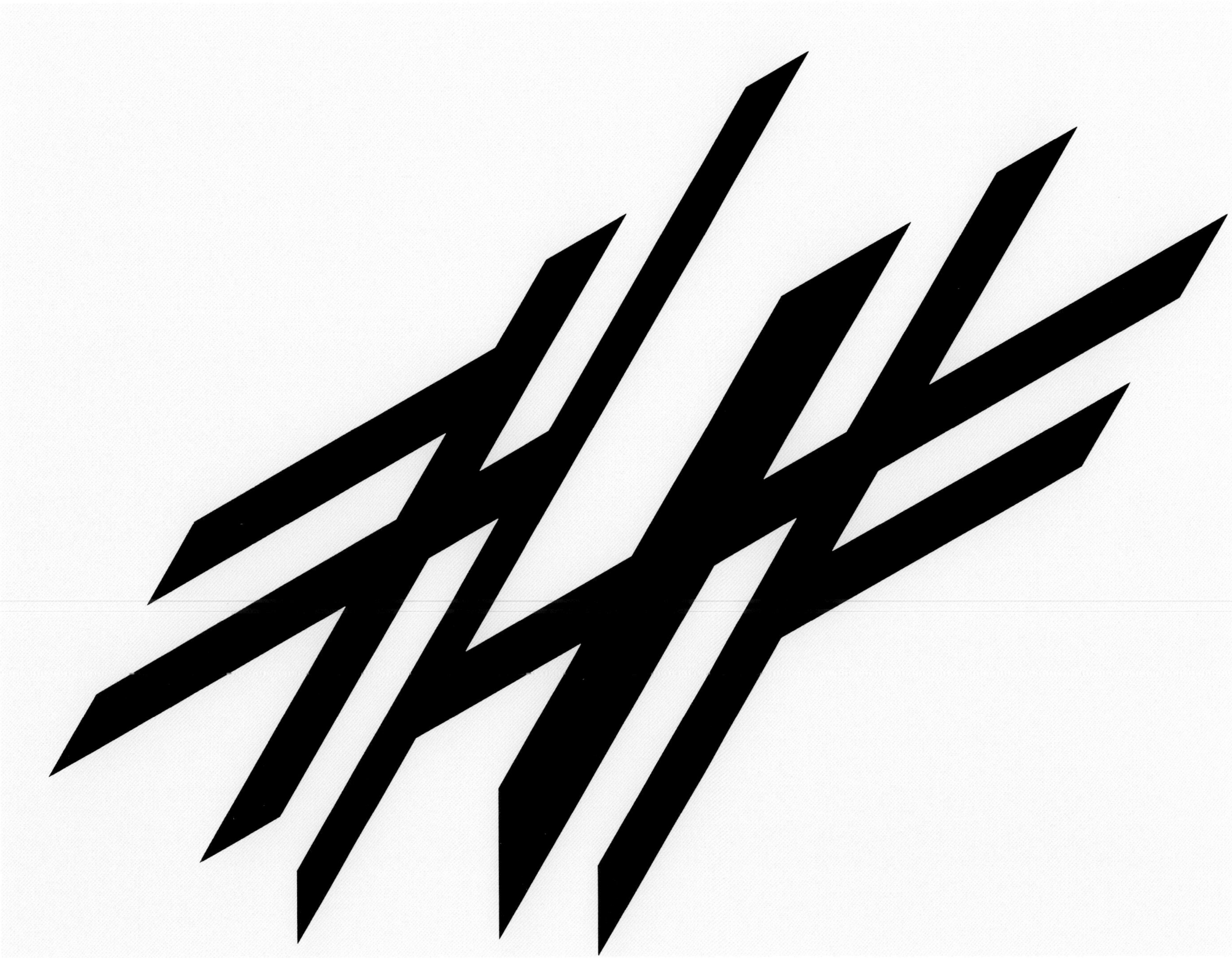

Marcellina, 2013, 29 5/8" x 78", Acrylic on Canvas

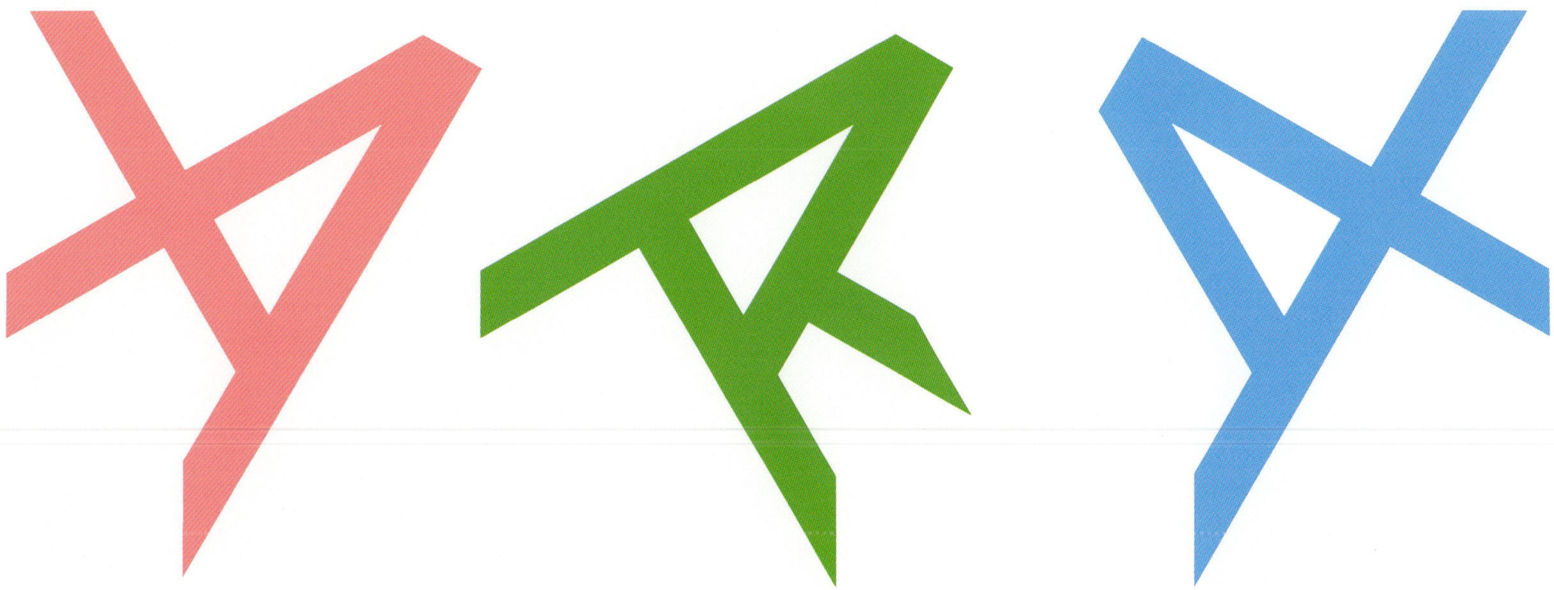

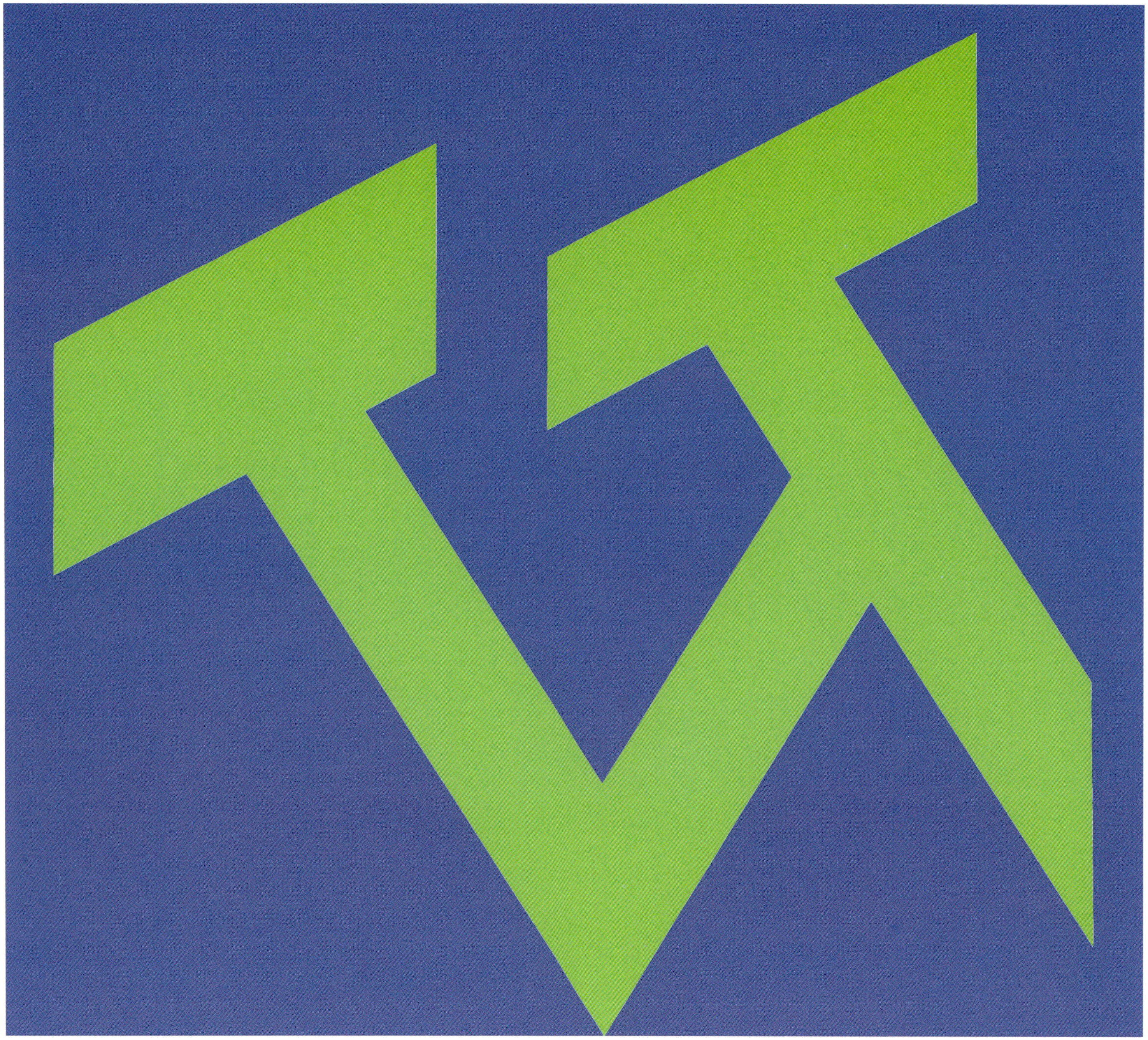

Theodosius, 2013, 54 1/2" x 54 7/8", Acrylic on Canvas

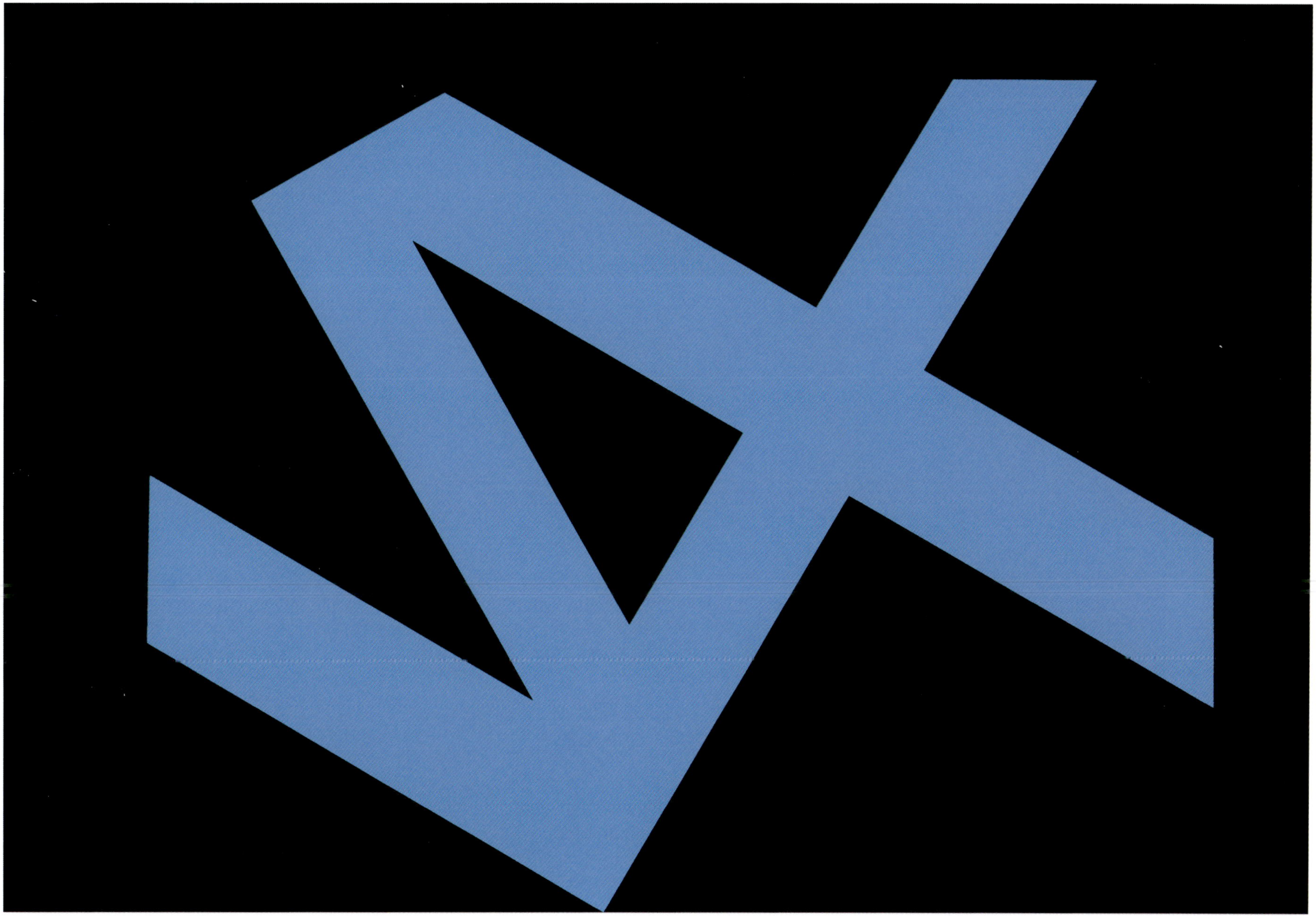

Canisius, 2013, 49 3/8" x 70 3/8", Acrylic on Canvas

SUSANNA, 2012, 56" X 62 3/8", ACRYLIC ON CANVAS

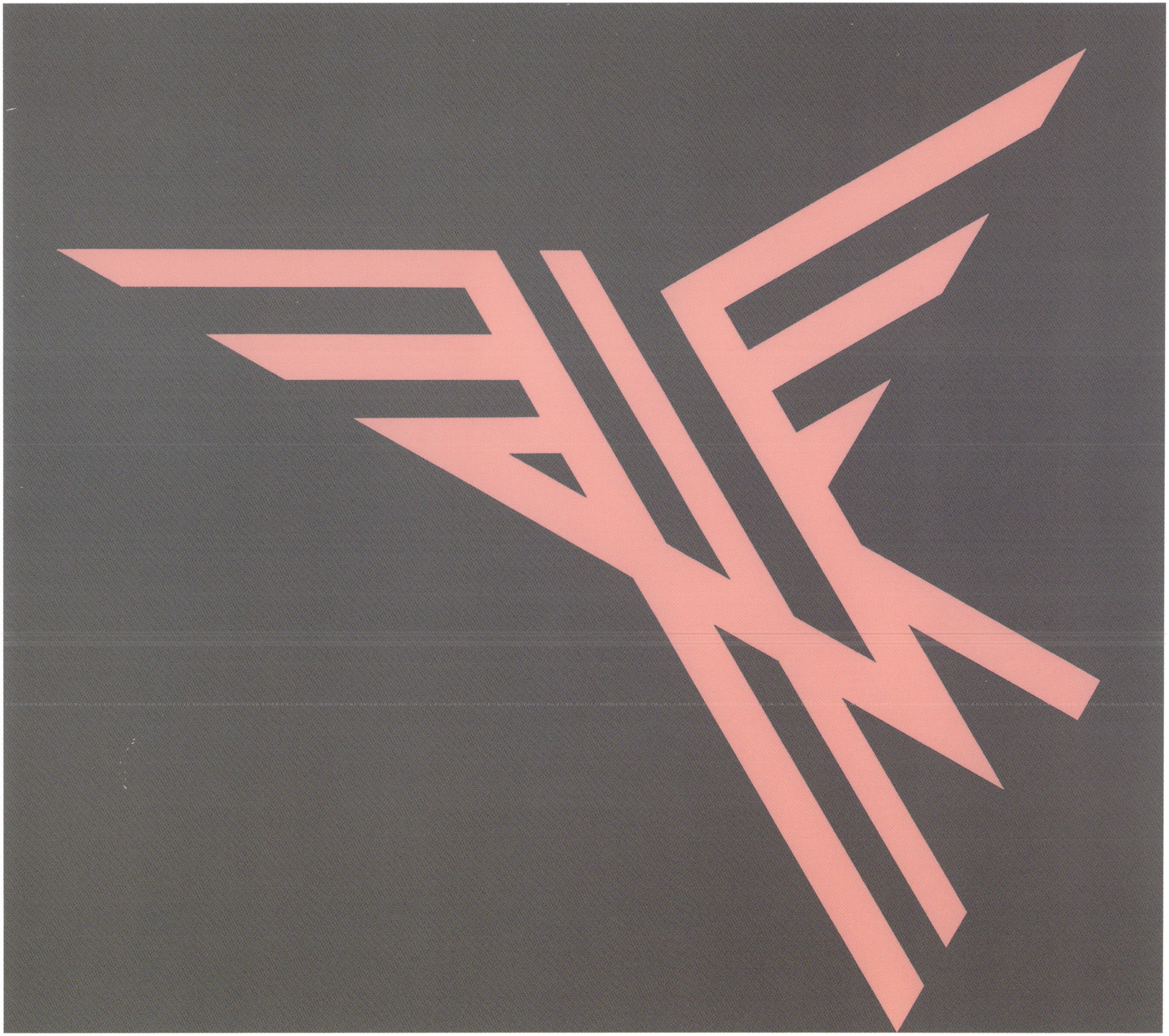

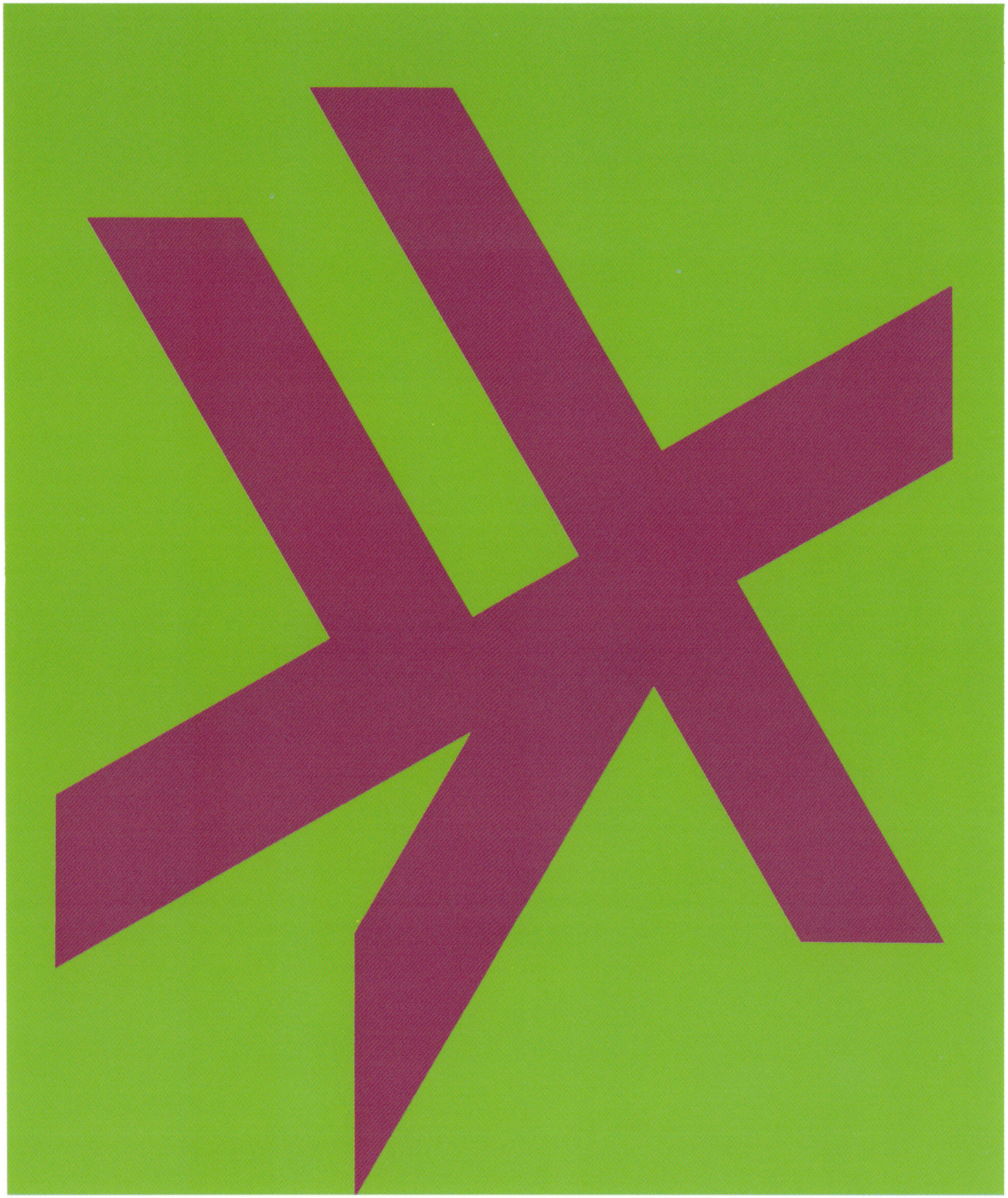

Childermas, 2013, 63" x 52 1/8", Acrylic on Canvas

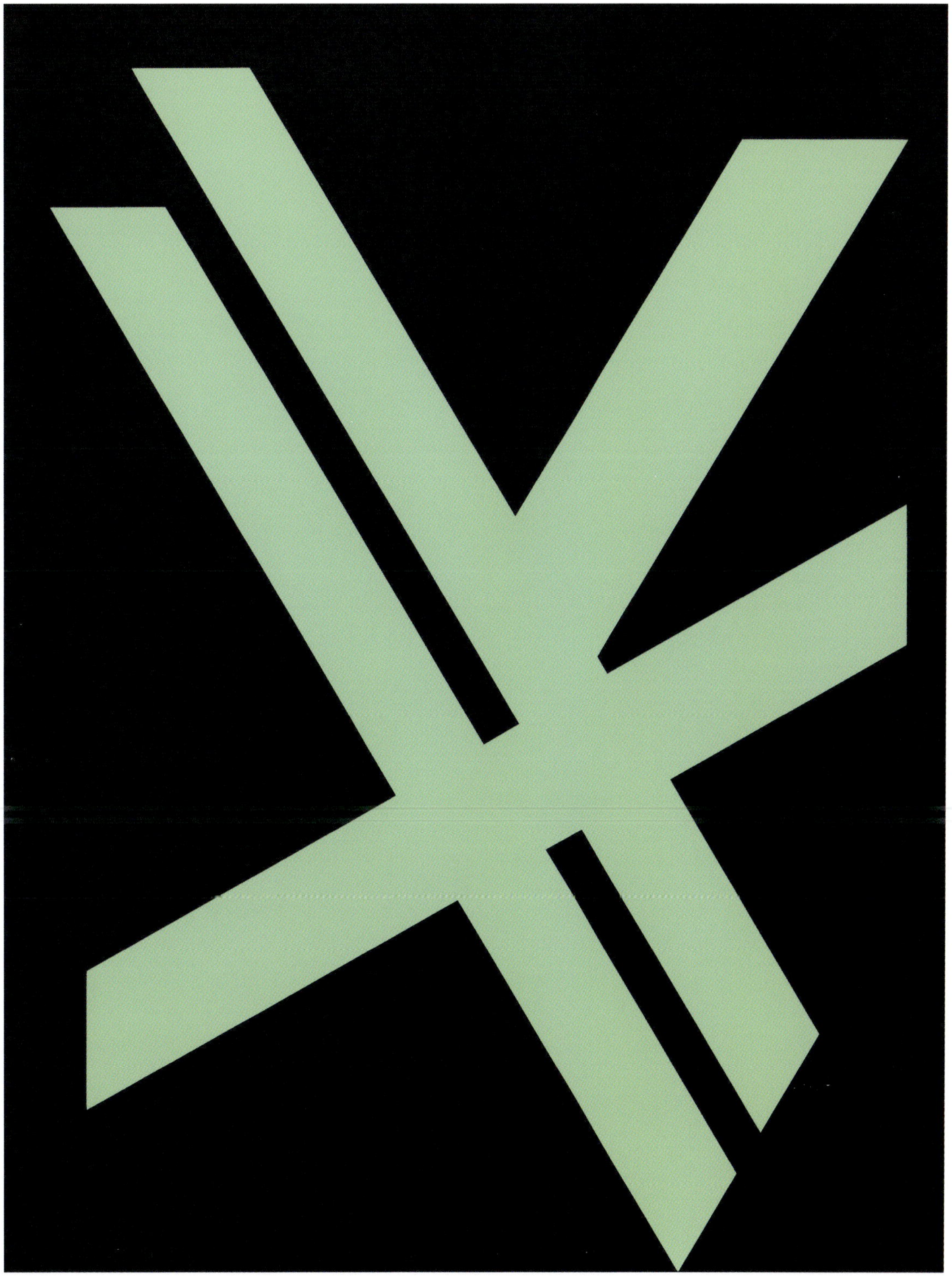

Alexander, 2014, 61 1/2" x 44 1/2", Acrylic on Canvas

Waudru, 2014, 48 5/8" x 56 1/8", Acrylic on Canvas

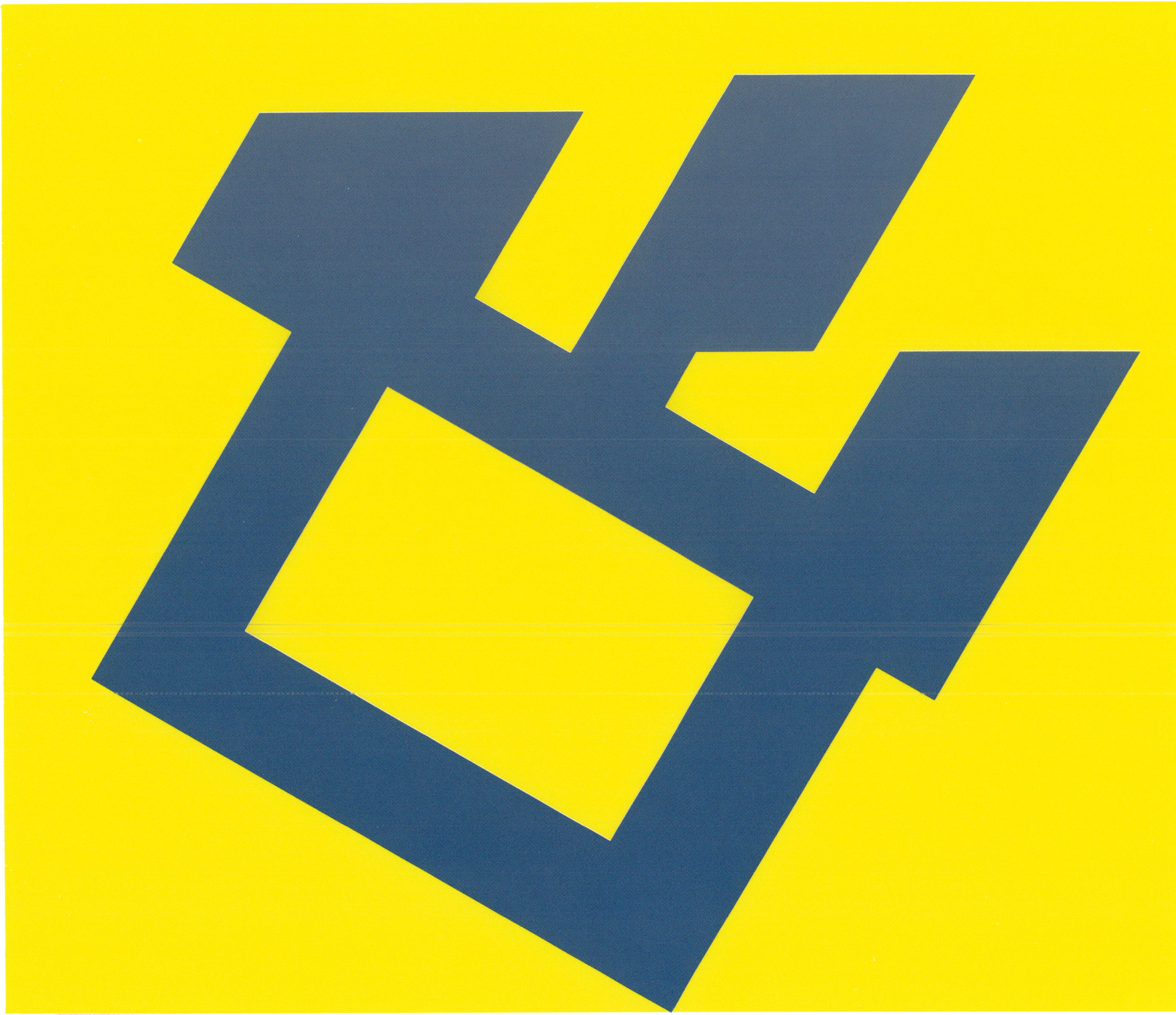

Tomas, 2014, 62" x 74 1/2", Acrylic on Canvas

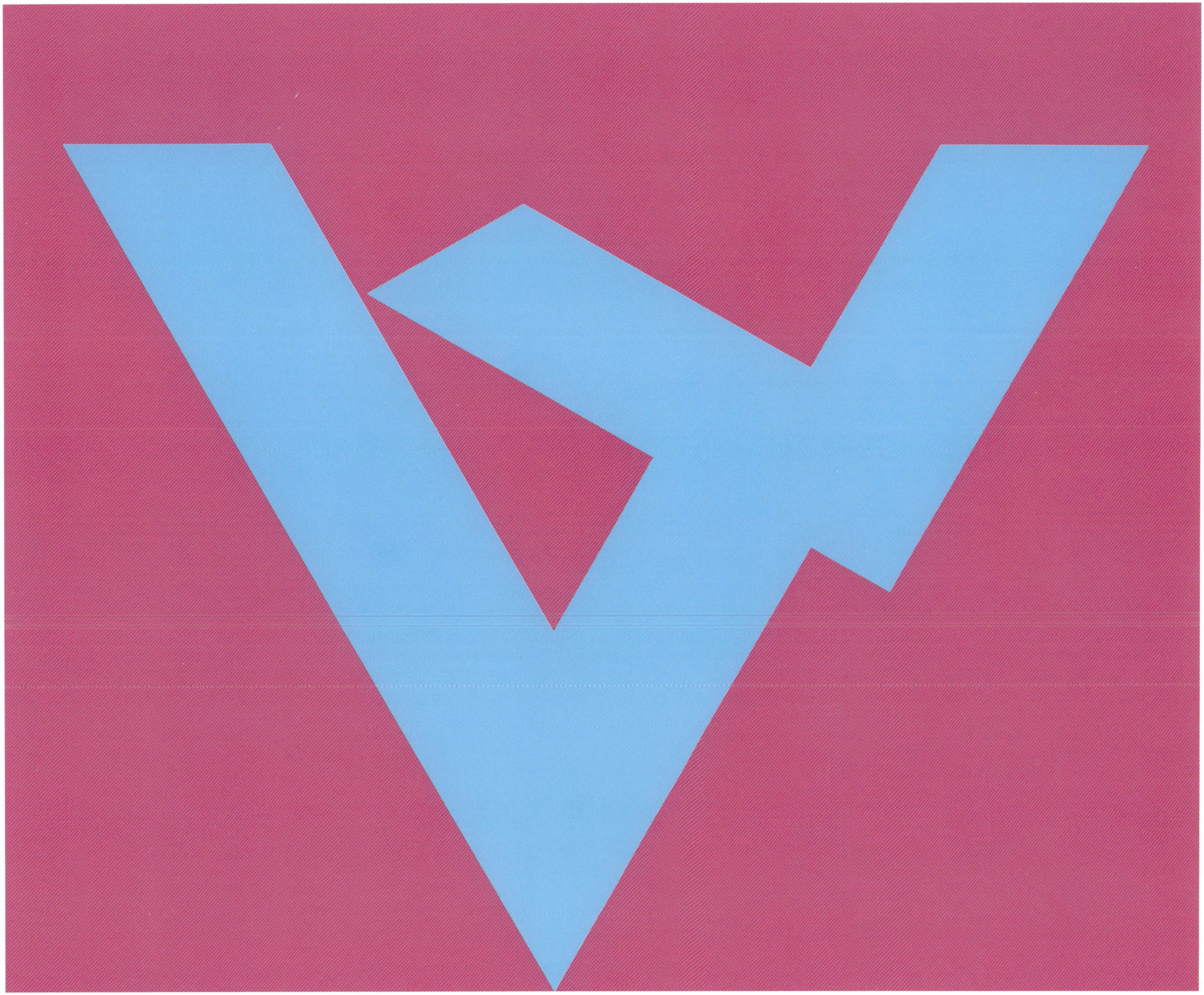

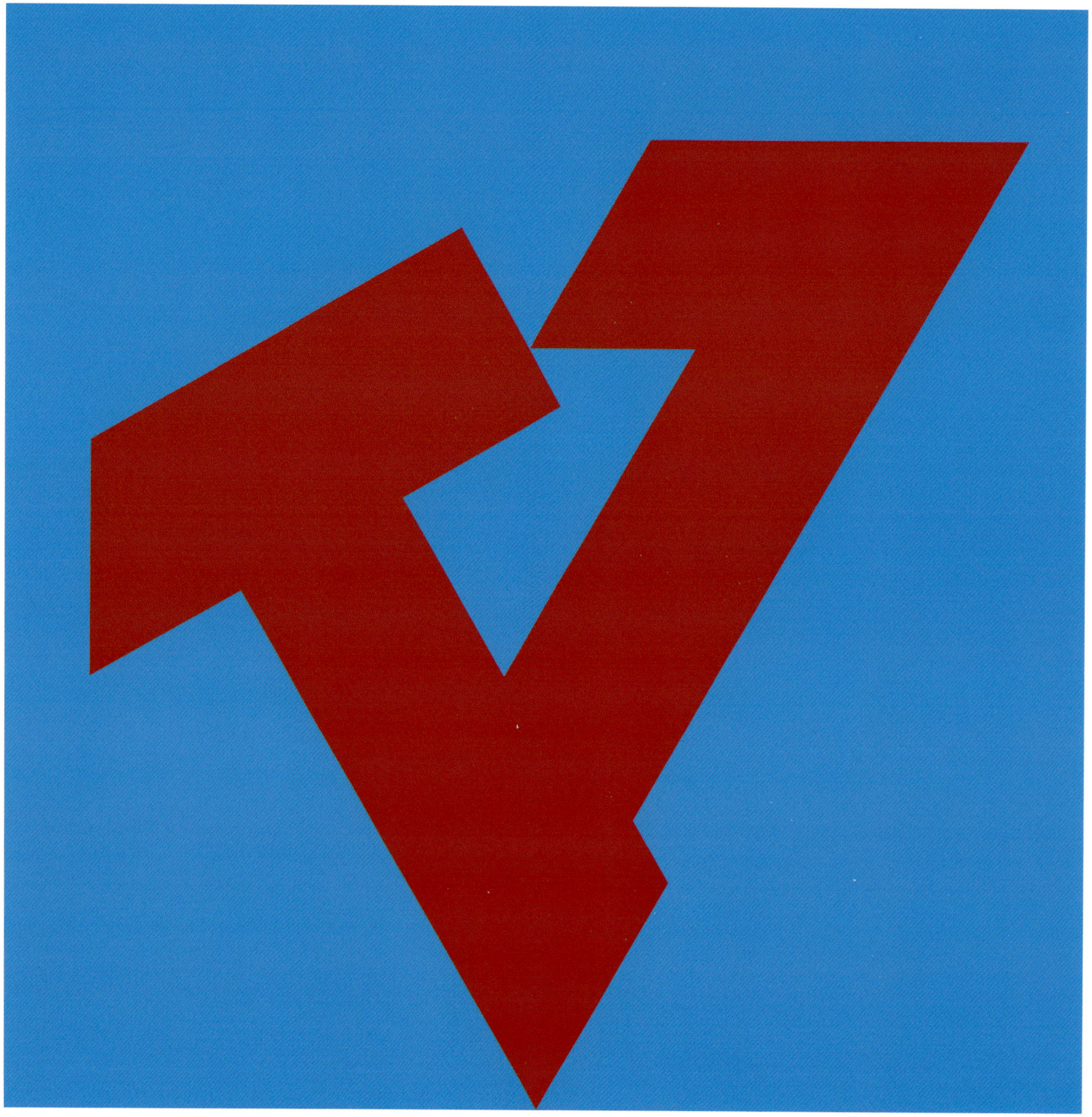

Alban(2), 2016, 21 5/8" x 21", Acrylic on Canvas

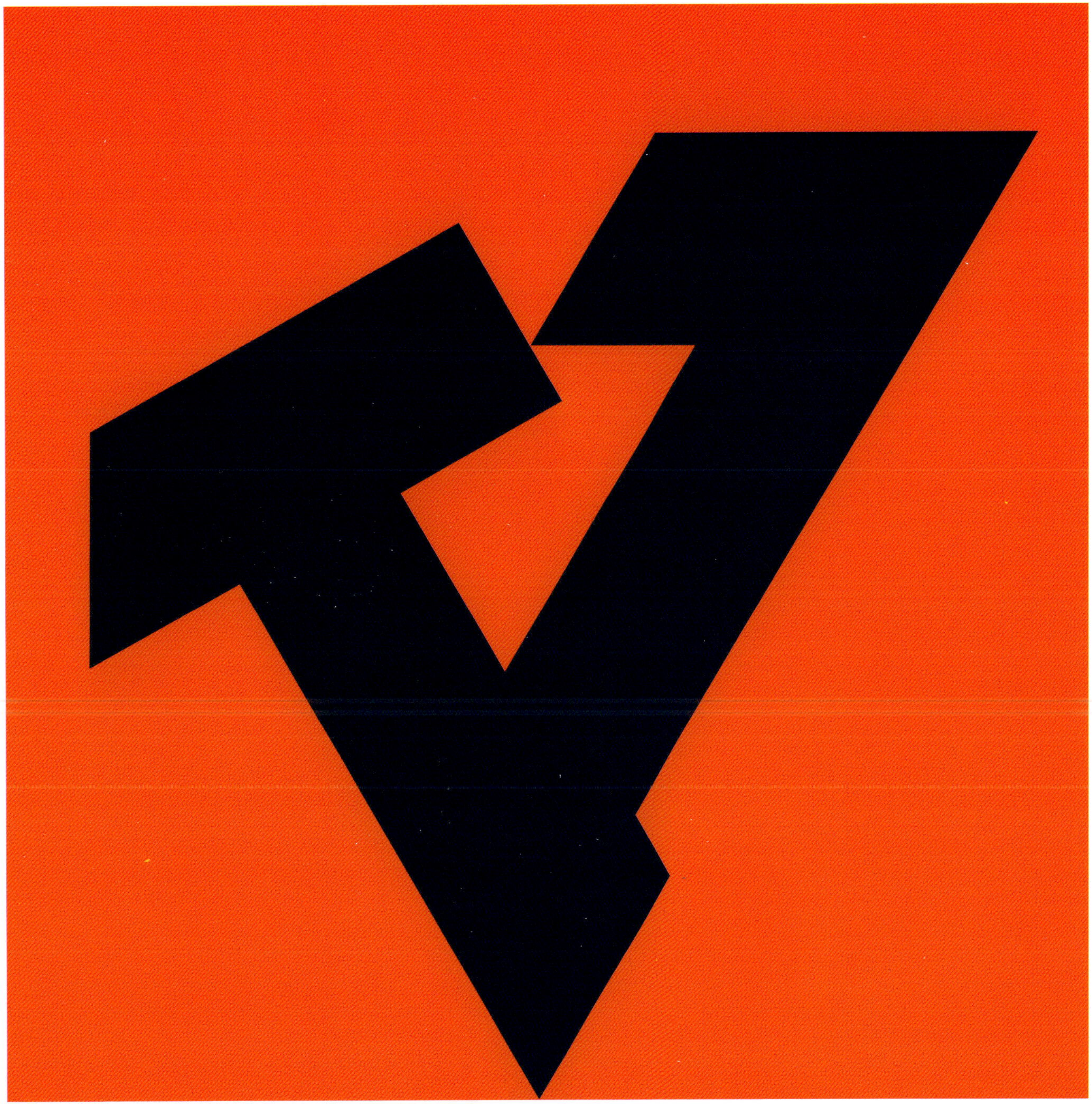

Alban, 2016, 51 5/8" x 50 3/8", Acrylic on Canvas

Geremar, 2016, 37 3/4” x 66”, Acrylic on Canvas

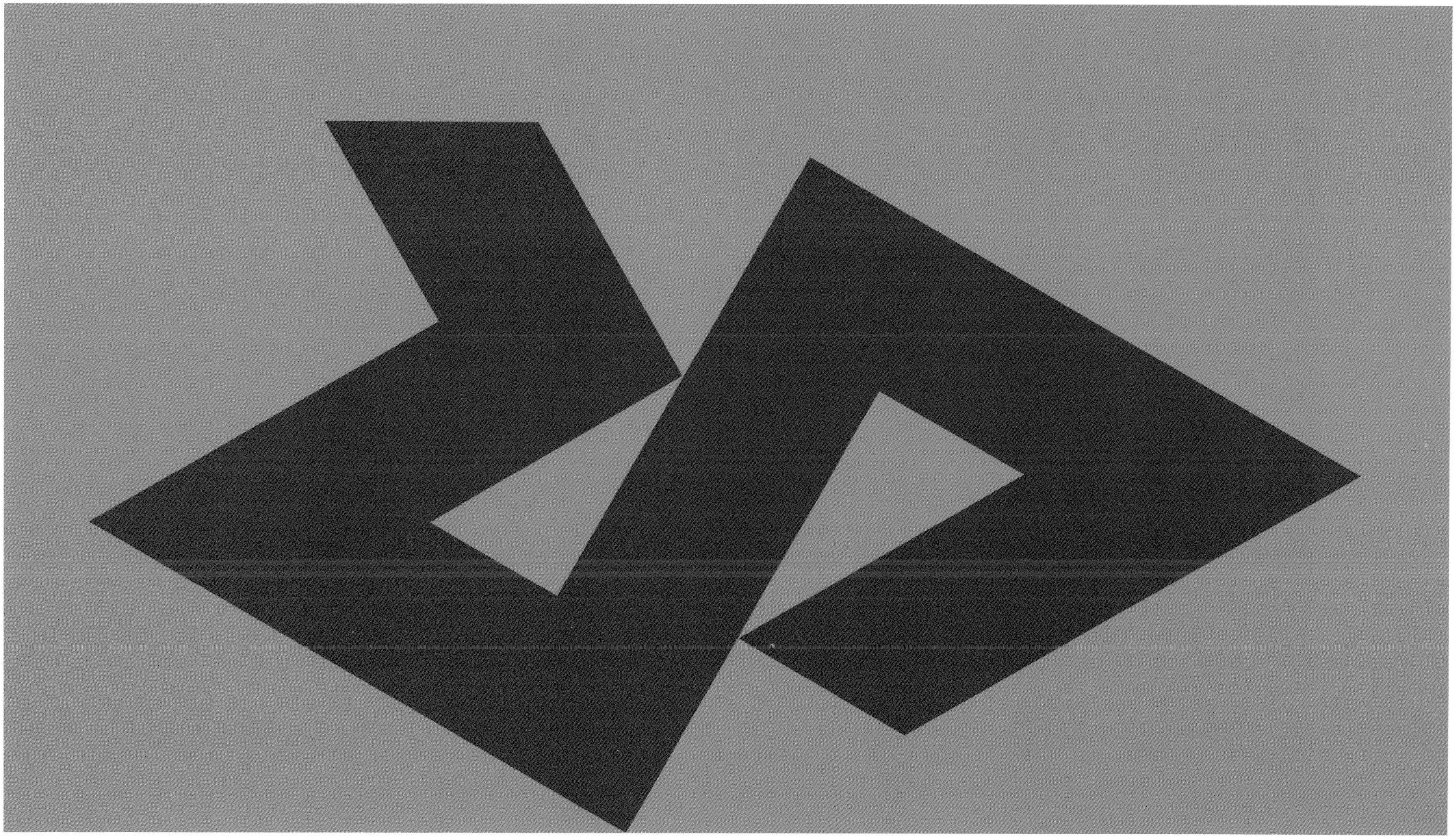

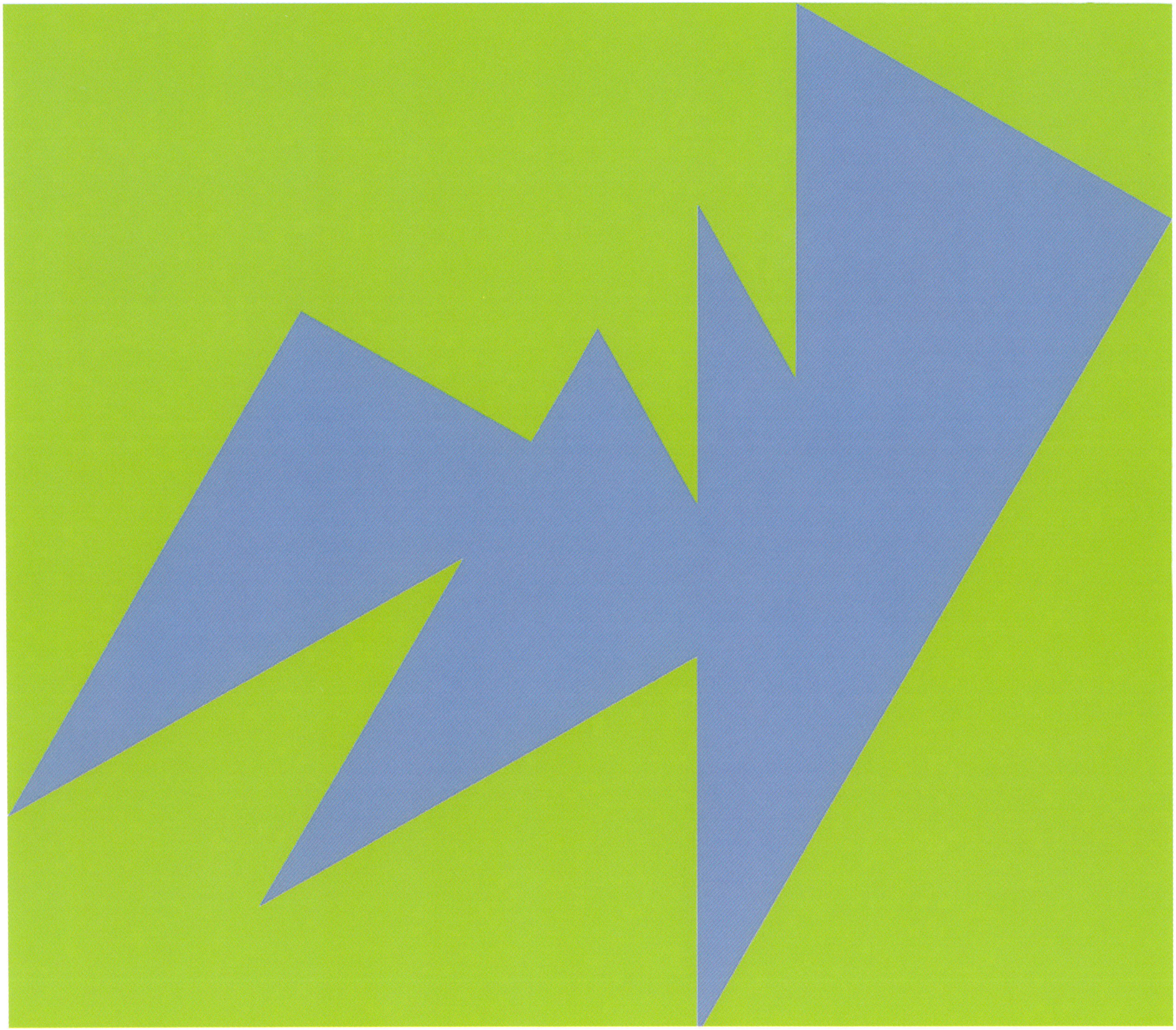

ANTHERUS, 2017, 24 1/2" x 27 5/8", Acrylic on Canvas

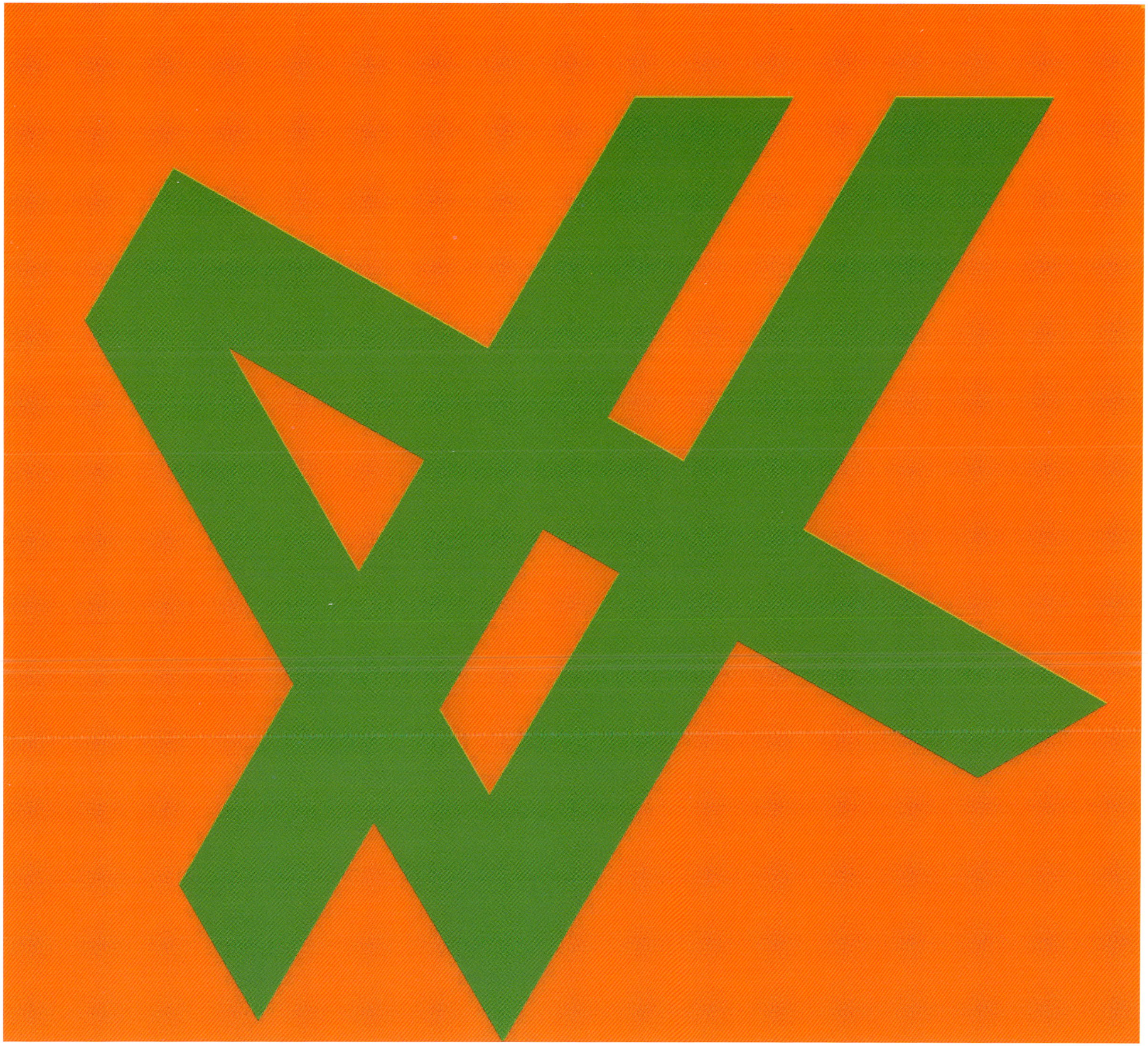

Vincent, 2017, 52″ x 56 1/2″, Acrylic on Canvas

Pontian, 2017, 53 1/4" x 79 1/8", Acrylic on Canvas

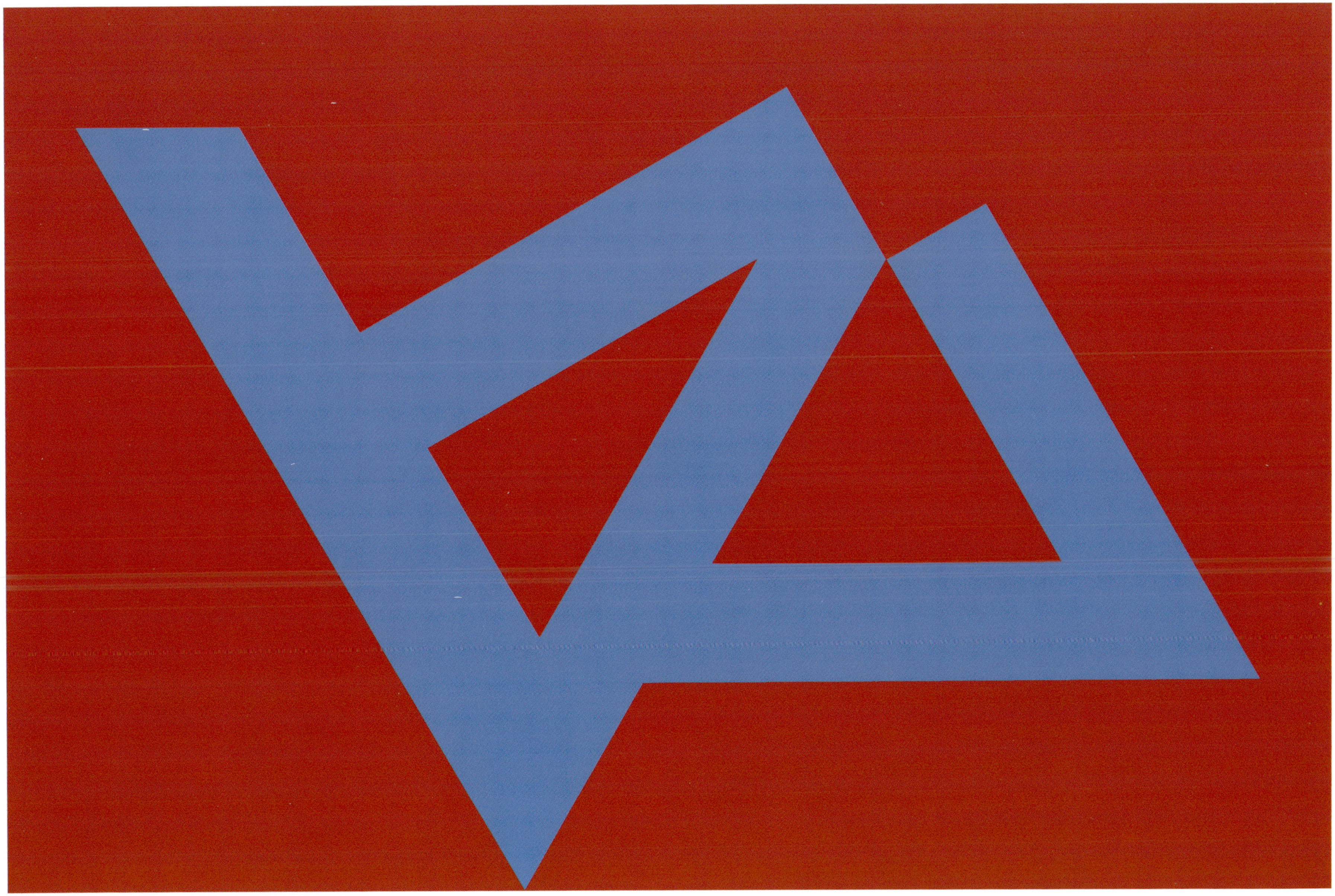

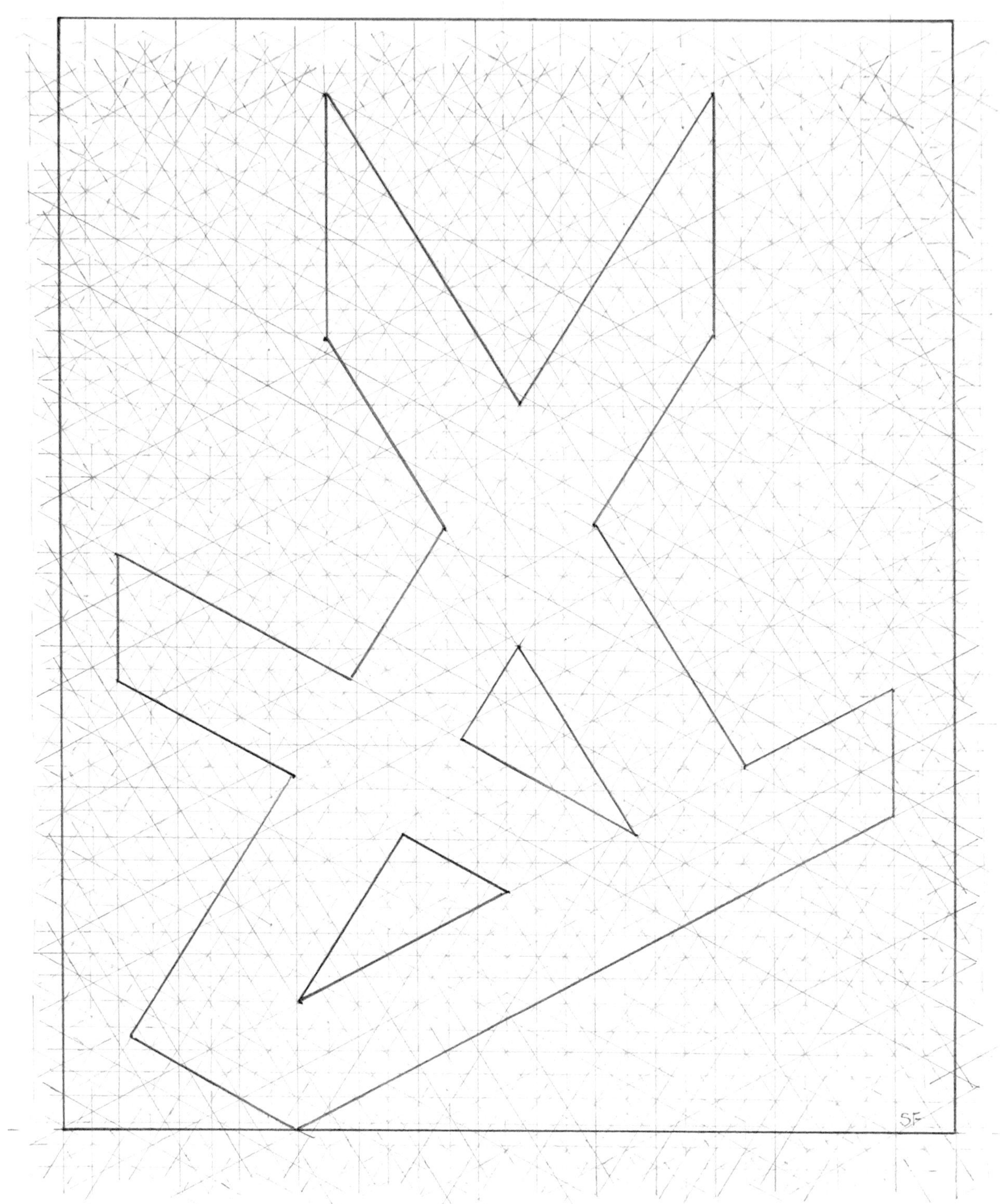

5-19-2017, 2017, 8 1/2" x 6 1/4", Graphite on Paper

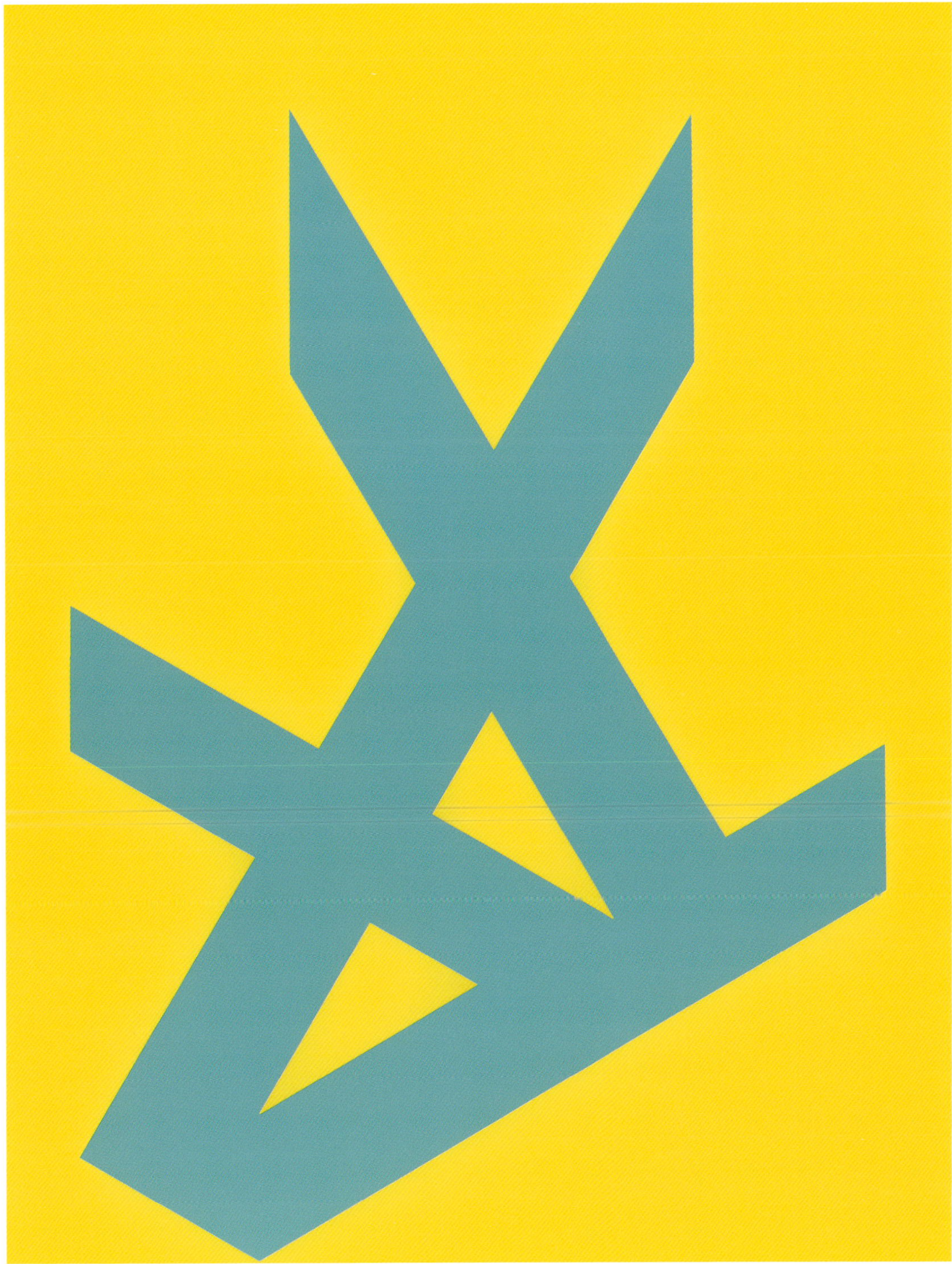

Alcuin, 2017, 65 3/8" x 48 3/8", Acrylic on Canvas

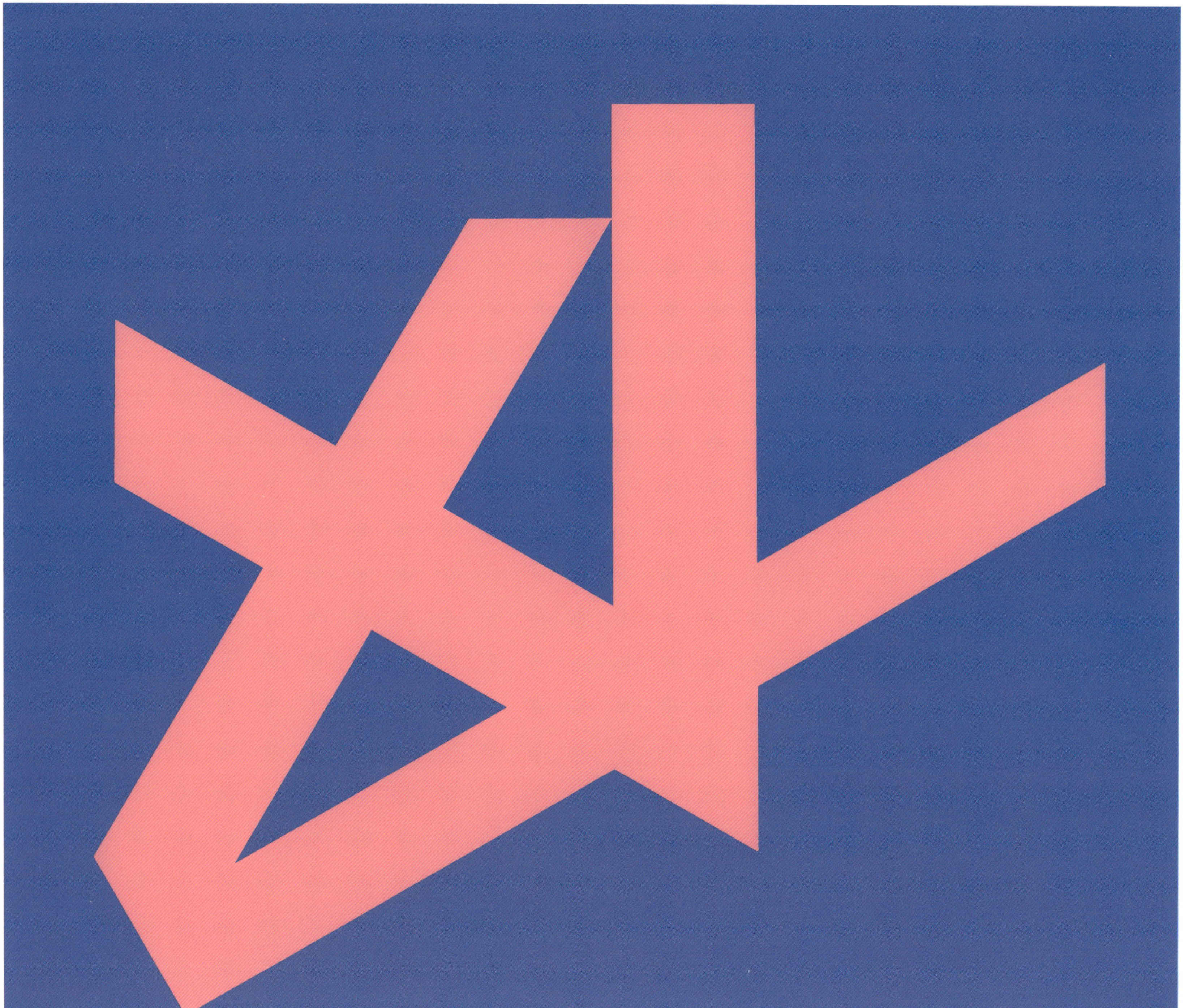

Martinian, 2017, 55 5/8" x 64", Acrylic on Canvas

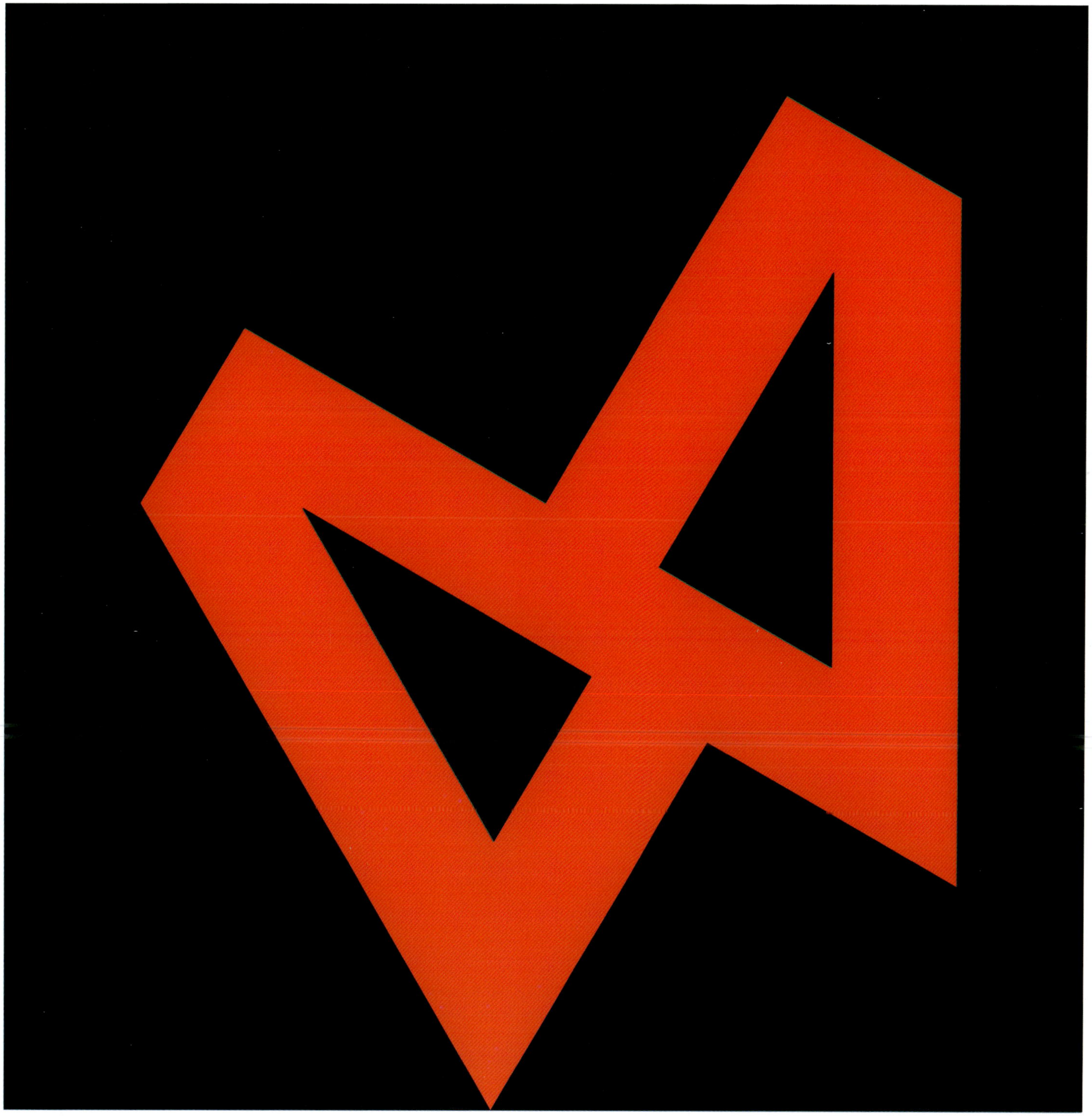

Titus, 2018, 35 5/8" x 34 5/8", Acrylic on Canvas

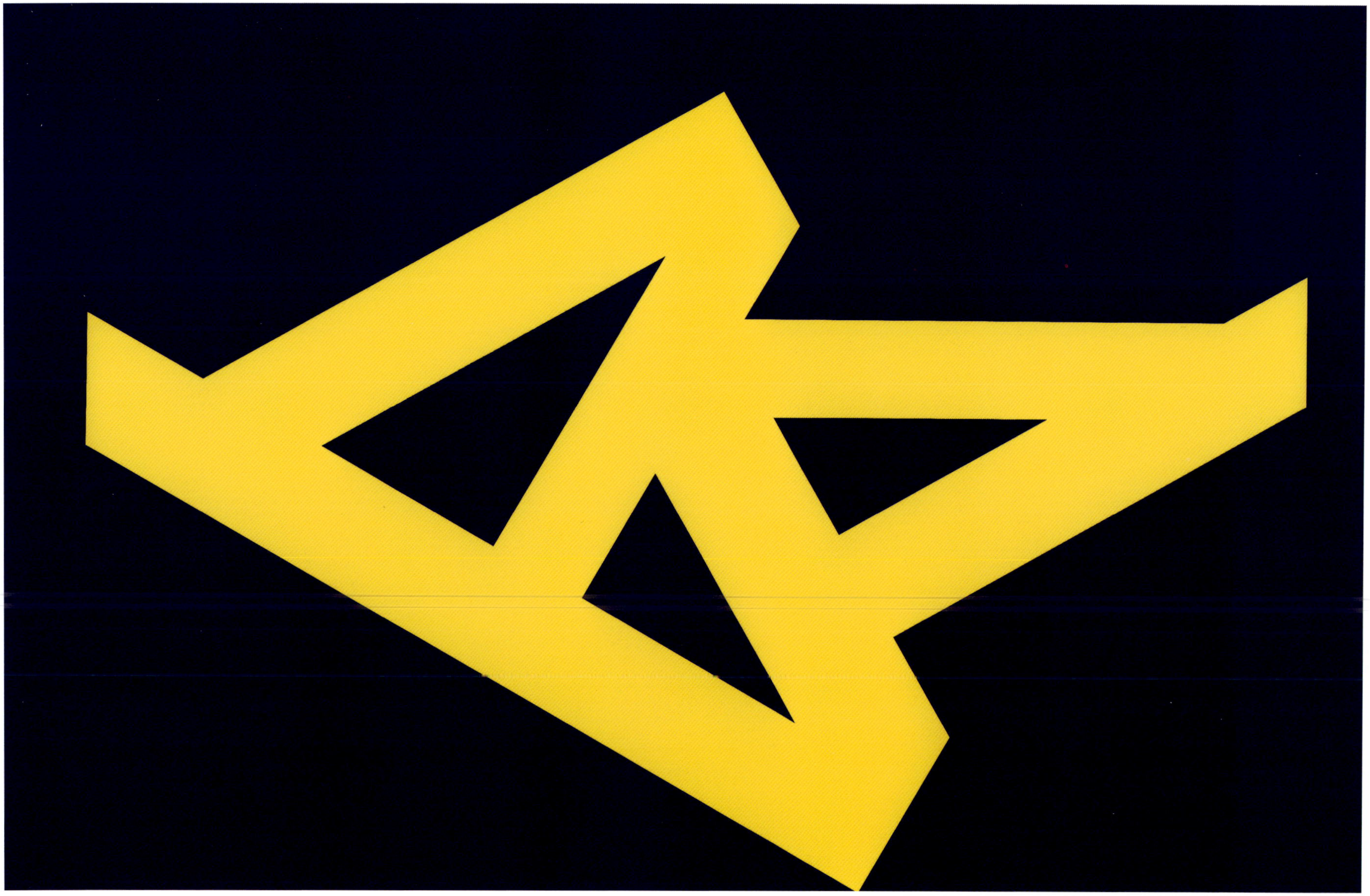

Valerian, 2017, 40 5/8" x 62 1/8", Acrylic on Canvas

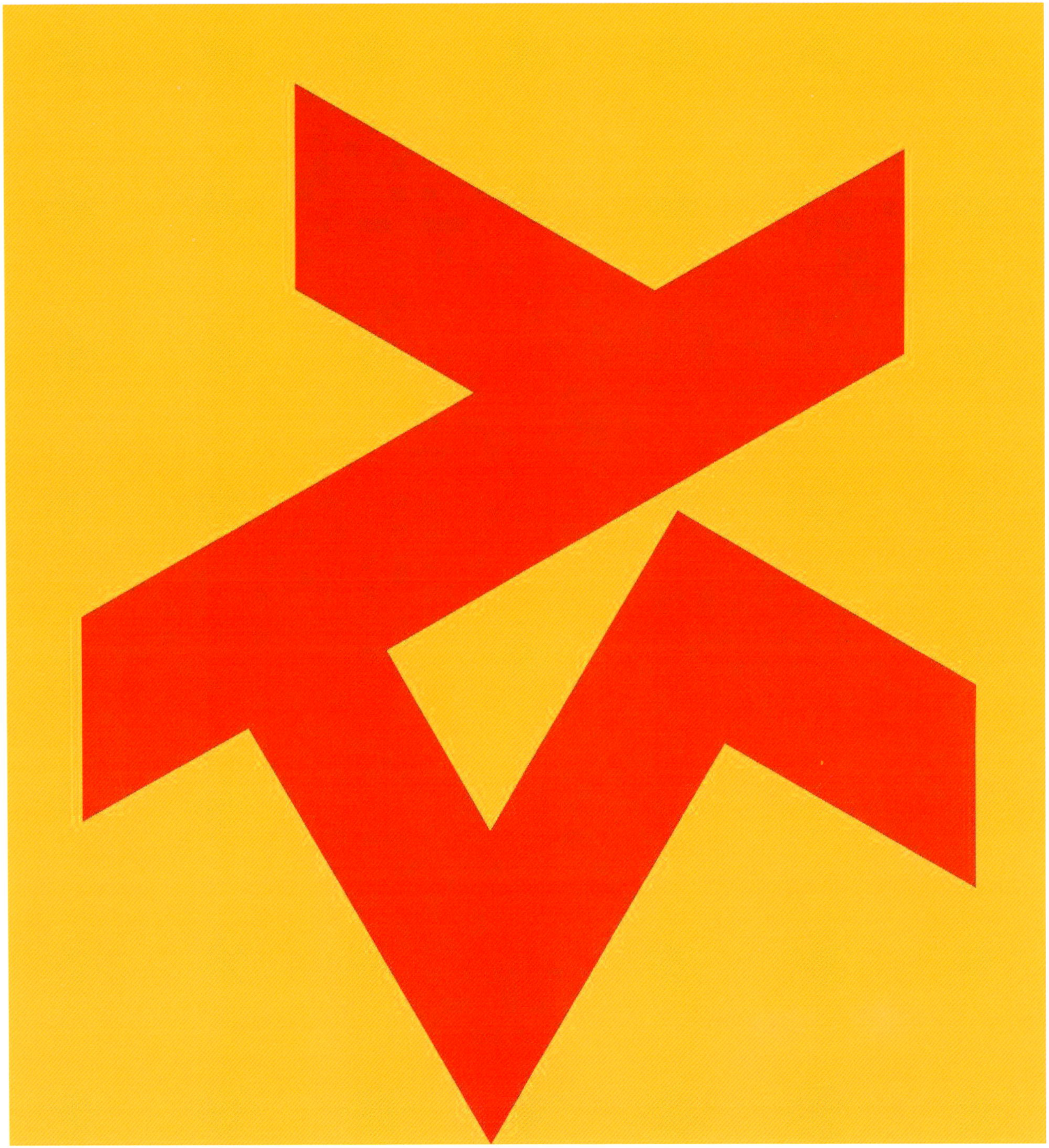

Isaac Jogues, 2018, 62 1/8" x 56 1/4", Acrylic on Canvas

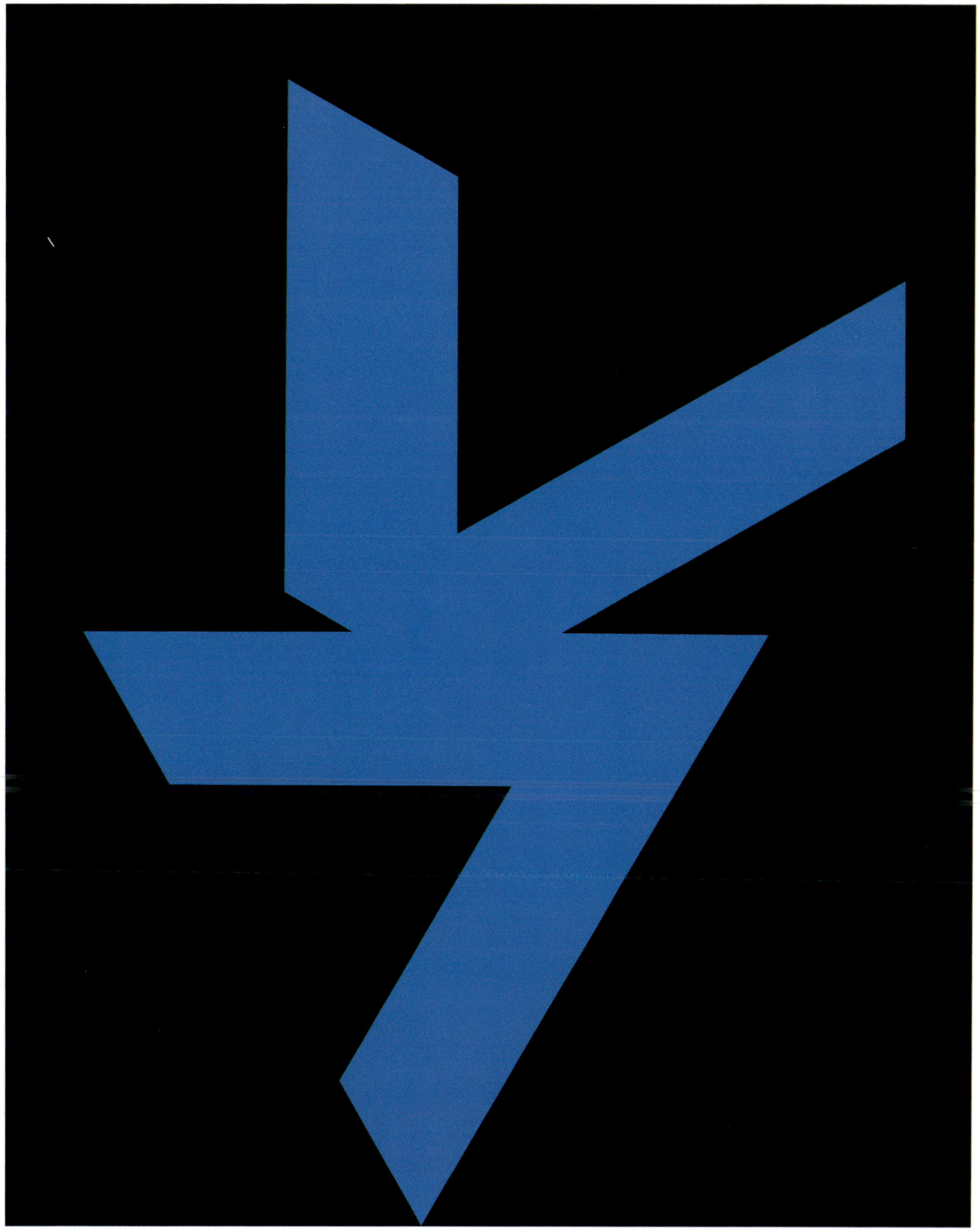

Eleutherius, 2018, 68 7/8" x 54 3/8", Acrylic on Canvas

Selected Bibliography

1969 *A Grandness of Intent* by F.D. Cossitt
Virginian-Pilot, October 26, 1969

1986 *Show's Juror Used Hard Criteria*
by Robert Merritt
Richmond-Times Dispatch, March 30, 1986

2000 *Art by Sal Federico: Sharp, Vibrant*
by Elise Freda
Middletown Times Herald-Record,
February 3, 2000

2000 *Theory for Gallerygoers* by Jed Perl
The New Republic, March 20, 2000

2002 *Learning Curves* by Lance Esplund
Modern Painters, Vol. 15, Number 1,
Spring 2002

2003 *Unity and Variety* by Jed Perl
The New Republic, January 27, 2003

2003 *Talent at the End of the Line: Perfecting Abstract Equipoise* by Mario Naves
New York Observer, February 24, 2003

2003 *Salvatore Federico at Amos Eno*
by Lance Esplund
Art in America, October, 2003

2004 *Angular Gestures* by Mario Naves
New York Observer, June 14, 2004

2006 *Salvatore Federico: Recent Paintings*
by Maureen Mullarkey
The New York Sun, May 18, 2006

2006 *In Good Shape* by Mario Naves
New York Observer, May 24, 2006

2008 *The Enigmatic Paintings of Salvatore Federico* by Lance Esplund, New York, 2008

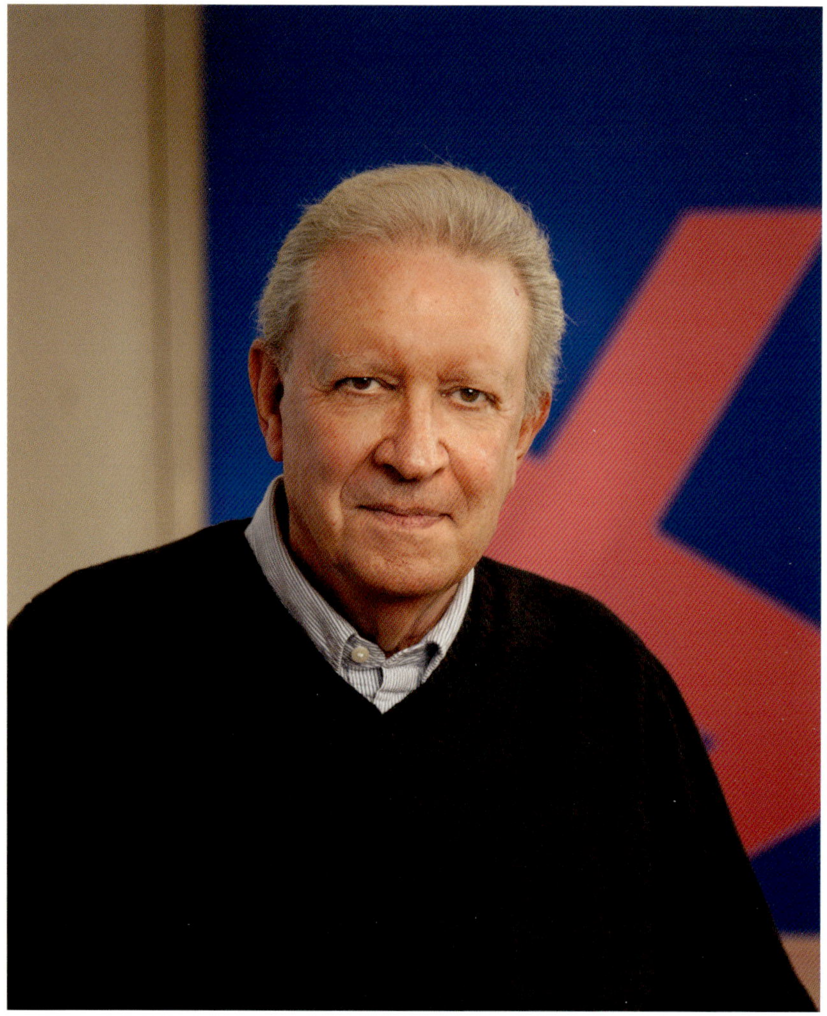

Salvatore Federico, 2017

Selected Solo Exhibitions

2019 *Recent Paintings*
Walter Wickiser Gallery, New York, NY

2014 *Recent Paintings*
Nancy Margolis Gallery, New York, NY

2010 *Recent Paintings & Drawings*
George Billis Gallery, New York, NY

2009 *Recent Paintings & Drawings*
George Billis Gallery, Los Angeles, CA

2006 *Recent Paintings & Drawings*
George Billis Gallery, New York, NY

2004 *Recent Paintings & Drawings*
George Billis Gallery, New York, NY

2003 *Recent Paintings*
Amos Eno Gallery, New York, NY

2001 *Recent Paintings & Drawings*
Amos Eno Gallery, New York, NY

2000 *Recent Paintings & Drawings*
SAI Gallery, New York, NY

1999 *1999 Recent Paintings & Drawings*
Delaware Valley Arts Alliance,
Narrowsburg, NY

1969 *Recent Paintings*
Twentieth Century Gallery,
Williamsburg, VA

1966 *Recent Paintings*
Richmond Professional Institute,
Richmond, VA

Two-Person Exhibitions

1995 *Open Studio*
290 Lafayette Street, New York, NY

1992 *Recent Paintings*
Monty Stabler Gallery, Birmingham, AL

Open Studio
290 Lafayette Street, New York, NY

1991 *Open Studio*
290 Lafayette Street, New York, NY

1990 *Open Studio*
290 Lafayette Street, New York, NY

Group Exhibitions

2019 *Art on Paper 2019,*
Walter Wickiser Gallery, New York, NY

2016 *A Symposium,*
VanDeb Editions, Long Island City, NY

2002 *NY Art DC*
Gallery 10, Ltd., Washington, DC

2001 *Members Annual*
Liberty Museum, Liberty, NY
New York, New York
ARC Gallery, Chicago, IL

1998 *Members Annual*
Liberty Museum, Liberty, NY

1988 *Group Show*
John Davis Gallery, New York, NY

1987 *Roethke Arts Festival*
Lafayette College, Easton, PA

Group Show
44 Beard Street Gallery, Brooklyn, NY

1986 *Selections 34*
The Drawing Center, New York, NY

1983 *Big Plum–Big Apple*
Kuban Gallery, Cleveland, OH

1982 *Colors At An Exhibition*
Caulfield Gallery, New York, NY

Group Show
Van Wickle Gallery, Lafayette College, Easton, PA

Regulars
T.A.B. Gallery, New York, NY

1981 *Faculty '81 Exhibition*
College of the Arts, The Ohio State University, Columbus, OH

Group Show
Toni Birckhead Gallery, Cincinnati, OH

Visiting Artists & Faculty
Hopkins Hall Gallery, The Ohio State University, Columbus, OH

1980 *Been Here & Gone*
1708 East Main Street Gallery, Richmond, VA

New Talent
A.M. Sachs Gallery, New York, NY

1940–1980
Virginia Museum of Fine Arts, Richmond, VA

1974 *Painting & Printmaking Faculty Show*
Anderson Gallery, Virginia Commonwealth University, Richmond, VA

1972 *Southeastern Artists Traveling Exhibition*
Painting Invitational, Southeastern Center for Contemporary Art, Winston-Salem, NC

Painting & Printmaking Faculty Show
Anderson Gallery, Virginia Commonwealth University, Richmond, VA

Ten Years Ago Painting Invitational
Jewish Community Center, Richmond, VA

35th Semi-Annual Juried Show
Southeastern Center for Contemporary Art, Winston-Salem, NC

Irene Leach Memorial Exhibition
Chrysler Museum, Norfolk, VA

1971 *34th Semi-Annual Juried Show*
Southeastern Center for Contemporary Art, Winston-Salem, NC

Virginia Museum Biennial Juried Exhibition
Virginia Museum of Fine Arts, Richmond, VA

Robinson House Additions
Painting Invitational, Virginia Museum of Fine Arts, Richmond, VA

Painters' Independent Enterprise Dimock
Gallery, George Washington University, Washington, DC

VCU Painting & Printmaking Faculty Show
Richard Bland College, Petersburg, VA

Works on Paper
Invitational Exhibition, Jewish Community Center, Richmond, VA

VCU Painting & Printmaking Faculty Show
Virginia State College, Petersburg, VA

1970 *Artists & Architects–An Interaction*
American Institute of Architects Convention, Fredericksburg, VA

Group Drawing Show
Twentieth Century Gallery, Williamsburg, VA

33rd Semi-Annual Juried Show
Southeastern Center for Contemporary Art, Winston-Salem, NC

32nd Semi-Annual Juried Show
Southeastern Center for Contemporary Art, Winston-Salem, NC

Painters' Independent Enterprise Drawings
The Gallery of Modern Art, Fredericksburg, VA

Painters' Independent Enterprise
The Carillon Museum, Richmond, VA

3rd James River Juried Show
Mariners Museum, Newport News, VA

1969 *Painters' Independent Enterprise Prints,*
Chapman College, Orange, CA

Print Invitational
Jewish Community Center, Richmond, VA

Twelve VCU Faculty
Drawings and Prints, Windsor Gallery, Richmond, VA

Painting Invitational
Jewish Community Center, Richmond, VA

Painters' Independent Enterprise
The Carillon Museum, Richmond, VA

1968 *Sculpture Invitational*
Jewish Community Center, Richmond, VA

1965 *Undiscovered Artists*
Jewish Community Center, Richmond, VA

1963 *Group Show*
Lee Gallery, Alexandria, VA

1962 *Group Show,*
Associated Artists Gallery, Washington, DC

Index

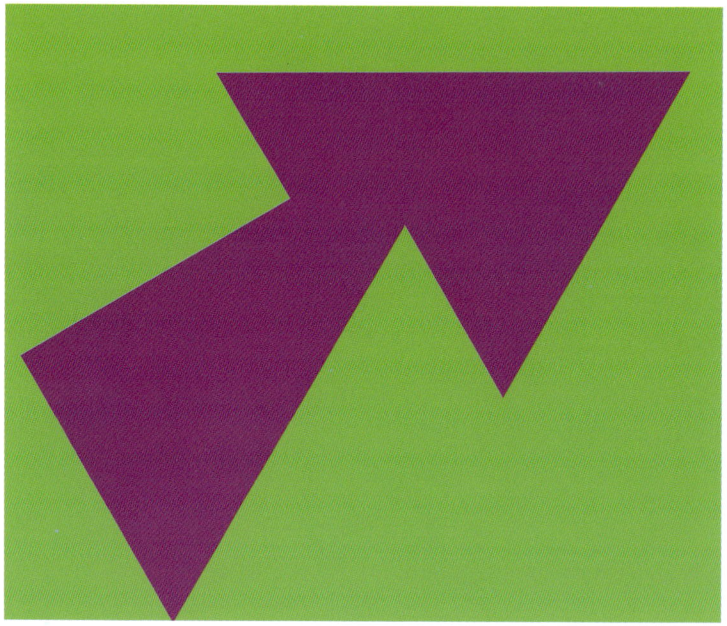

ELEAZAR, 1998, 22 1/8" x 25 11/16", OIL ON CANVAS

Credits

Photography Credits

© Photography by

S. Allison	12
Washington-Post	13
M. Wall	14, 15
L. Wall	20, 21
David Lubarsky	22, 25
Dana Duke	7, 122

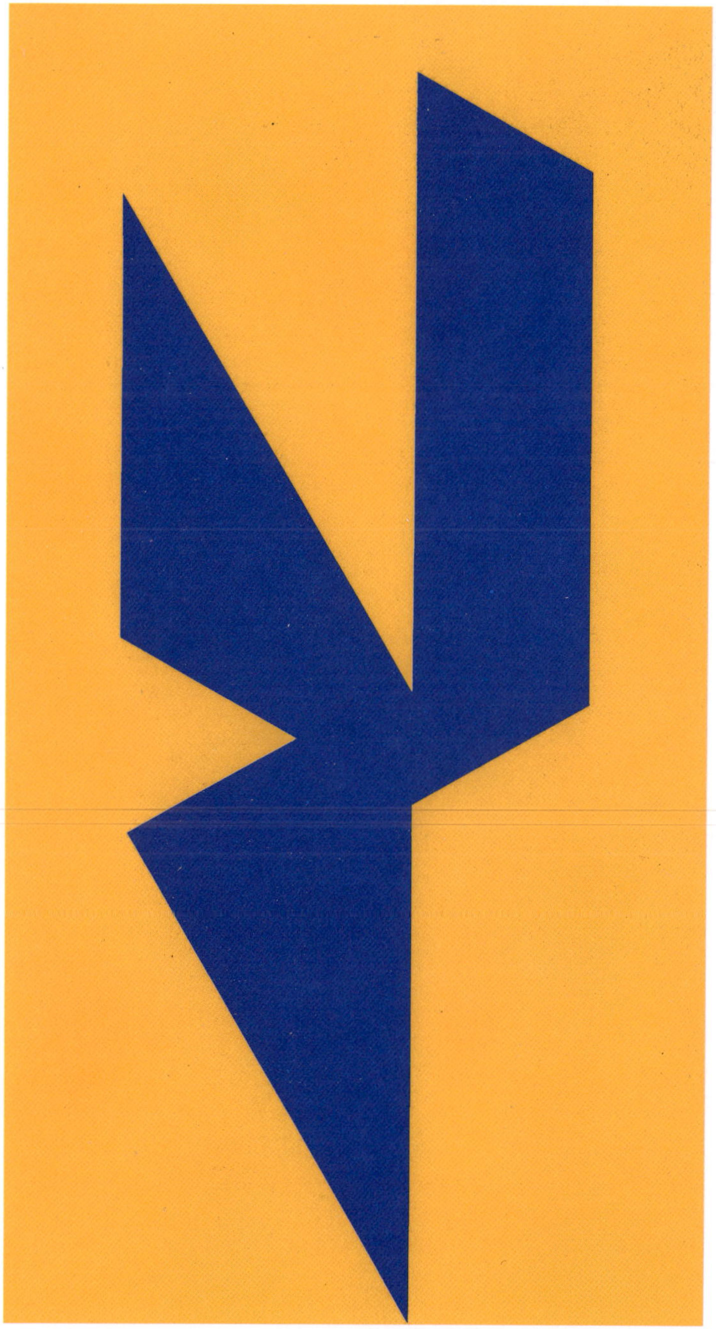

Proterius, 2002, 73 1/4" x 38 1/2", Acrylic on Canvas